Photo by Lotte Jacobi

MAY SARTON

By AGNES SIBLEY

Lindenwood College

 213

Twayne Publishers, Inc.   ::   New York

Preface

The poet who is also a novelist may easily become identified with one of the genres to the neglect of the other. May Sarton, who places chief value on her poetry, is best known as a novelist. But her work is all of a piece, for the poems and the novels abound in similar themes and images. The novels have an inwardness, a careful, sensitive rendering of subjective experience that one would expect from a good poet; and the music of her prose is such that one is constantly tempted to read it slowly or aloud. Anywhere in her fiction one might find such a passage as this one from her first volume of autobiography: "In my mind's eye I see my mother running through those two years . . . across dappled light and shadow, always green leaves over her head and sunlight splashing down, alone with the cries of birds and the swift shallow river" (29).

It is likely that Miss Sarton's prose fiction has enlarged the audience for poetry. Many who might never open a book of poems find, in her novels, a heightened sense of life—the poet's awareness of sensuous experience, the colors, sounds, textures of the world, and also the poet's vivid realization of the difficulty, pain, and joy of being human. She explores with honesty the complex world of human relationships and the deep, wordless struggles that are usually made articulate only in poetry. Her work also shows a constant concern with Europe as well as with America, for she was born in Belgium of a Belgian father and an English mother. Although her parents brought her to the United States when she was four years old and she later became a naturalized American citizen, her tie with the "old country" has remained; it is both an emotional force and a theme in her writing. Characters in some of her novels, are, when flying across the Atlantic, suddenly plummeted into a strange new culture and feel a surge of exhilaration or dismay. What are the differences between Europe and America? Why do Americans often feel defensive when they are abroad, and yet as if they were somehow coming home? Miss Sarton's writing throws light on these and related questions.

The present study, the first book on May Sarton that has appeared, undertakes to show the unity of all her writing. After the first chapter, which summarizes her life as she recounts it in two books of autobiography and several autobiographical poems, the main body of her work is surveyed. The second chapter discusses her poems and her ideas about the nature of poetry as she has given them in articles, in lectures at colleges, and the novel, *Mrs. Stevens Hears the Mermaids Singing*. The third and fourth chapters deal with her novels, but reference is made now and then to the poetry to show related themes. The last chapter summarizes the chief themes that have been set forth and evaluates her achievement as a writer.

I am grateful to Dean Howard Barnett of Lindenwood College for his constant interest in and encouragement of this study.

AGNES SIBLEY

Lindenwood College
St. Charles, Missouri

Contents

Chronology

1912   May Sarton born in Wondelgem, Belgium, May 3; parents, George and Mabel Elwes Sarton.

1916   Came with parents to the United States. (Naturalized in Boston, 1924.)

1917–   Shady Hill School, Cambridge, Massachusetts.
1926

1926–   The High and Latin School, Cambridge, Massachusetts;
1929   graduated 1929.

1930–   Apprentice at Eva Le Gallienne's Civic Repertory Theatre,
1936   New York; member First Studio and Director of Apprentice Group, Civic Reportory.

1933–   Founder and director, Apprentice Theatre (New School for
1936   Social Research); director of Associated Actors Theatre Inc. (Hartford, Conn., Wadsworth Athenaeum).

1937   *Encounter in April*, poetry.

1937–   Taught creative writing and choral speech at the Stuart
1940   School, Fenway, Boston.

1938   *The Single Hound*, novel.

1939   *Inner Landscape*, poetry.

1944–   Office of War Information, script writer for documentary
1945   films about the United States to be sent overseas.

1940–   Extensive lecturing on poetry in colleges of the United
1950   States.

1945   Awarded the Golden Rose of the New England Poetry Society; Poet in Residence at the summer session of Southern Illinois University, Carbondale.

1946   *The Bridge of Years*, novel.

1948   *The Lion and the Rose*, poetry.

1950   *Shadow of a Man*, novel.

1950–   Briggs-Copeland Instructor in Composition, Harvard Uni-
1953   versity.

1951– Lecturer, Breadloaf Writers' Conference.
1952

1952 *A Shower of Summer Days,* novel.

1953 *The Land of Silence,* poetry; Lucy Martin Donnelly Fellow, Bryn Mawr College.

1953– Lecturer, Boulder Writers' Conference.
1954

1954 Guggenheim Fellowship in Poetry.

1955 *Faithful Are the Wounds,* novel; Honorary Phi Beta Kappa, Radcliffe College.

1956 *The Fur Person,* novel.

1957 *The Birth of a Grandfather,* novel.

1958 *In Time Like Air,* poetry; Fellow, American Academy of Arts and Sciences; Honorary Doctor of Letters, Russell Sage College.

1959 *I Knew a Phoenix,* autobiography.

1959– Phi Beta Kappa Visiting Scholar.
1960

1960– Danforth Visiting Lecturer, College Arts Program.
1961

1960– Lecturer in Creative Writing, Wellesley College.
1964

1961 *Cloud, Stone, Sun, Vine,* poetry, and *The Small Room,* novel; The Johns Hopkins Poetry Festival (lecture and reading of poetry).

1964 *Joanna and Ulysses,* novel.

1965 *Mrs. Stevens Hears the Mermaids Singing,* novel; Poet in Residence, Lindenwood College, fall semester.

1966 *Miss Pickthorn and Mr. Hare,* novel, and *A Private Mythology,* poetry.

1967 *As Does New Hampshire,* poetry, and *Plant Dreaming Deep,* autobiography.

1967 National Foundation of the Arts and Humanities Grant.

1968– Twelve monthly articles—general title "Homeward," *Family*
1969 *Circle* magazine.

1969 *The Poet and the Donkey,* novel.

1970 *Kinds of Love,* novel.

1971 *A Grain of Mustard Seed,* poetry; Honorary Doctor of Letters, New England College.

1972 *A Durable Fire,* poetry.

CHAPTER *1*

Two Worlds

IN *I Knew a Phoenix,* subtitled *Sketches for an Autobiography,* Miss Sarton relates the story of her early life until the beginning of her career as a poet. The title of this book comes from a line of W. B. Yeats, "I knew a phoenix in my youth, so let them have their day." The implication is of a mysterious glory in one's past that can hardly be communicable, and such is the tone of Miss Sarton's first volume of autobiography. Her youth was a time of intensity, excitement, and exploration—a reaching out to life with both hands. Though she knew difficulties and disappointments, the chief impression left by her book is of wonder and joy.

Part I, entitled "The Fervent Years," tells of her parents. Her father, George Sarton, is shown first as a rather solitary little boy in a gloomy old house in Ghent, learning to make his own decisions and growing into "a young man full of intellectual curiosity and innocent arrogance" (17). He was, from the first, independent and self-assured, cherishing unorthodox opinions and idealistic longings to improve the world. This "shy, eccentric, passionate young man" hoped at first to become a poet and novelist, for "he was in a perpetual fever of ideas and feelings that had no outlet" (40). In time, he made friends with other radical young people, including a group of idealistic working girls, one of whom was Mabel Elwes, whom he eventually married.

Miss Sarton's account of her mother begins with the chapter called "A Wild Green Place," describing the two years that the child Mabel spent on a farm in Wales while her parents were in Canada. A lyrical and at times painful tale (for the child suffered from the neurotic rages of an unbalanced woman at the farm), it depicts the sensitivity and courage of Mabel Elwes and, incidentally, how much she was like the young man she was to marry. They met in Ghent, where Miss Elwes went to study art after her father's death. The courtship extended over several years, and its course was not always smooth; but in 1910 "these two passionate, sensitive, opinionated, strong characters came to admit that they could not live without each other . . ." (62).

In 1912, May Sarton was born. She was to be the only child, but she and her parents felt that in a sense she was a "twin" of another entity, the journal *Isis,* a review "devoted to the history of science and civilization" which her father founded in the same spring that she was born. He later dedicated one of his books to his wife, "Eleanor Mabel, mother of those strange twins, May and Isis" (69). By 1912 her father's purpose was set in the direction he would go: he was to become famous as the author of the monumental *Introduction to the History of Science* and to achieve international fame as a scholar. His conviction that he could not do his work in Belgium, once the 1914–18 war had begun, led the Sartons to the painful decision that they must leave their beautiful country home in Wondelgem for England. They took with them only the few things they could carry, and even George Sarton's precious notes were buried in a metal box in the garden; and "we set out for the border, passing through the advancing army" (79). Miss Sarton remembers none of this, but she imagines what the departure must have been like: "There had hardly been time to take a last look at the garden, at the beloved house, lying there so airy and sunny and quiet in its orchard green. Did my mother look back one last time at the long protecting wall that had sheltered all she loved for such a very brief time? At the great beech, standing inviolate, its leaves shining in the sun?".

The Sartons lived as refugees in England and later in New York and Washington, during which time her mother designed furniture and clothes to help meet the family's expenses; and her father learned English and searched for a job that would provide freedom to write his history of science. At last, with financial help from the Carnegie Institute, George Sarton was able to settle with his family in Cambridge, Massachusetts, where he was given space in the Widener Library in exchange for teaching half a course at Harvard University.

Miss Sarton tells of finding, some years after her parents had died, a copy of Walt Whitman's *Leaves of Grass* inscribed "George from Mabel, August 31st, 1910." And she thinks of how her parents came, "so poor and hopeful" to the New World, where her father's dream could finally take on reality: "Whitman's belief in a generous humanism that could encompass all mankind was really not so far from George Sarton's vision of the healing, unifying power of the history of science—not of one science but of all sciences, and not of one nation but of all nations from the beginning of time" (98). Both her parents' deep involvement in life was communicated to Miss Sarton as something precious, something which finds expression in her own work—the novels and poetry that she, instead of her father, has published.

I *Education*

In the second part of *I Knew a Phoenix,* "The Education of a Poet," the account of two schools that she attended, the emphasis is again on fervor, caring about life. As she grew up, the passionate concern of her teachers influenced her. At Shady Hill School in Cambridge, which used unorthodox methods and stressed physical endurance as part of one's education, the enormous energy and imagination of Agnes Hocking, the founder of the school, created "a spiritual climate as bracing, as rich and unpredictable, as that of New England itself" (104). Mrs. Hocking taught poetry to the whole school and made the children see it as "heavenly madness" and "delight—the opening of a door into a land where everything on earth seemed gathered together and harmonized" (111). But not only poetry was superbly taught. In other subjects as well, the pupils learned to study for the pleasure and excitement of knowing. They came to think of books as friends, not as enemies; and they learned, Miss Sarton says, "to examine ideas, to take nothing for granted, to ask a great many questions, to consider, in fact, that we embodied the dignity of the inquiring mind, the sacred destiny of man" (140).

After this exhilarating experience, Miss Sarton found her years at the Cambridge High and Latin School an anticlimax; but in a school in Belgium, the Institut Belge de Culture Française, where she went for a year when she was twelve, she again had teachers who cared intensely about their work. Marie Gaspar, called Titi, aroused both terror and affection in her pupils. Marie Closset, who was to become the character Doro in Miss Sarton's first novel, imparted to her pupils something of her own deep love of literature. Her method was to instill, through reading aloud, an attitude of "enlightened homage" for the masters—"homage enriched by intellectual analysis but rooted in passion" (129).

II   *The Theater*

Miss Sarton did not attend college, and after high school her education was in her own hands. Although at times she has regretted not having gone to college, on the whole she feels it a gain; by discovering authors on her own, she has kept the excitement of exploration that was hers as a pupil at Shady Hill. Certainly the results of her own reading and study are comparable to what they might have been with a formal education, for she has taught at both Harvard University and Wellesley College and has lectured extensively at colleges throughout the United States.

The momentous decision not to attend college was brought about by her desire to become an actress. Two chapters in *Phoenix* deal with her work in the theater: for three years, she was a part of Eva Le Gallienne's Civic Repertory Theatre, and for another three years she directed her own theater group. When, after several "impossible campaigns," her company failed, she realized that her career had to take another direction. Her attitude toward what must have been a shattering experience is an example of her conviction that growth can come from destruction: "it is not a bad thing to have to face total failure at twenty-four. It toughens the spirit and makes one aware that . . . human beings have unquenchable resources within them" (193). She now turned her attention more seriously to the poetry that she had been writing for some years, and her first volume was published in 1937, the year after the failure of the theater company.

Even more important for her career than the "toughening" experience of failure had been the influence of Eva Le Gallienne. Miss Sarton explains why her imagination was so caught and stimulated by this great actress. It was not because of the glamor associated with her personality or with the theater; it was because in Miss Le Gallienne she found "tangible proof of what serving an art rather than using it for one's own ends can mean to those involved" (150). Miss Le Gallienne was another idealist (like George Sarton, Agnes Hocking, Marie Closset) who believed that the self must be submerged in something larger—that the giving of oneself is the secret of a significant life.

After her work in the theater had ended, Miss Sarton went to England for two visits; and the last chapter of the autobiography is "Two English Springs." She had several letters of introduction to British people, and on one occasion was bewildered and hurt by "English insularity," the attitude of amusement at all that she said and did because it differed from the English way. She began to feel then that she was an exile: "It was . . . the first disconcerting evidence that I belonged nowhere, a 'half-breed,' as I used to announce when I was a child, since my father was Belgian, my mother, English, and we lived in the United States. For many years I was to have this feeling of exile wherever I went, to be pulled back to Europe as 'home' and then to feel a stranger there, after all" (204).

But in the visits to England described in *Phoenix* the pain of the outsider is less noticeable than the tone of remembered joy. She recalls her meetings with Elizabeth Bowen and Virginia Woolf; her friendship with Julian and Juliette Huxley; and, above all, she remembers "Kot"—S. S. Koteliansky—another of the vital, energetic people who helped to mould her thought and character. In reading the autobiography, one sees how Miss Sarton came to admire intensity and individuality. A spirit of passionate rebellion against the mediocre runs through the book. Her father and mother were both highly individual; Shady Hill School was unconventional; her choice of the theater instead of college was anything but usual. An incident in her rather conservative high school is significant. When one of her teachers forbade her to write a theme on Henrik Ibsen, saying he was immoral, she rushed to the principal to protest but got no change in the decision. From then on she felt she no longer belonged to the school except for exterior conformity. "I became," she says, "a revolutionary outsider, holding Ibsen to my breast as perhaps a later generation would hold James Joyce" (141–42). Ibsen represented both a revolt against orthodoxy and a desire for the genuine. For the young poet of twenty-five, as she is when the book ends, idealism and intensity were combined.

III   *The Writer and Her Life*

When Miss Sarton decided to become a writer, she threw the whole of her energies into the work. A glance at the Chronology at the beginning of this book shows that, except for the years of World War II, she has published either poetry or fiction every year or two since 1937. These publications have been the chief events in an outwardly quiet life, spent mostly in Cambridge and in recent years in a village in New Hampshire. But she has kept in touch, through frequent traveling in Europe, with the world of her inheritance. And she has received numerous awards that testify to the excellence of her writing. In the years since 1937 she has also become a visiting lecturer and teacher of creative writing. Her recent book of poetry, *A Private Mythology,* is dedicated to her students at Wellesley College.

Some of Miss Sarton's poems are autobiographical; they refer to people and places mentioned in *Phoenix* and in the later autobiography called *Plant Dreaming Deep.* Of these people, those who have been most influential on her writing are her father and mother: "I must regard my whole life as an attempt to bring into focus and so be able fully to use the rich gifts I was given by a scholar father and an artist mother, each strong in his own right. I do not summon them, but they are there, pivotal tensions. Everything must be tested and questioned against their innocence, their passion, and my whole life a precarious balance between their two kinds of genius." [1]

Her father, as pictured in the poems, is not the shy young man of *Phoenix* but the world-famous scholar, toiling away at his history of science, the man with such clear values and sense of purpose that he "could tear up unread and throw away/ Communications from officialdom" because they took precious time from his work.[2] She praises his single-minded commitment in "The Sacred Order," a poem that mentions other fervent scholars like Michelet and Erasmus; they were not "detached" or "clever"—rather, they "suffered" and "burned" to find out and reveal the truth.[3] The title of the poem refers to a scholar's bringing order out of chaos, a work which she believes to be always the result of strong human feeling.

Two poems on her father appeared in *In Time Like Air,* a volume dedicated to his memory. In "My Father's Death" she compares herself to a ship which, having been built with care but for long "landlocked," is at last "stripped down" and launched on the sea. George Sarton's death is not seen as grievous or even sad but as mysteriously right; it means a "great grave moment" when she realizes she is now completely alone but still surrounded by his love. The diction is in keeping with his character as she has shown it elsewhere—words like "bountiful," "full grown," and "accomplished" show that he gave to her even in his death. The other poem, "A Celebration," is a strongly felt portrait of a great man, full of small details about his appearance and habits ("He bounced upon the earth he trod"). The staccato rhythm of the tetrameter lines is suited to the briskness of his movement. The poem begins: "I never saw my father old;/ I never saw my father cold." The "cold" refers both to the swiftness of his death and to his intensity as a scholar. The almost nursery-rhyme quality imparted by the simple diction and by the rhyming in couplets reflects his childlike innocence and uncomplicated devotion to his work. One of the most moving references is to his so often working late at night that people nearby found comfort in looking up to see his light burning. The poem ends with lines written by one of the neighbors after his death: " 'I did not know your father, but/ His light was there. I miss the light.' "

The Land of Silence is dedicated to the memory of Miss Sarton's mother. The tone of the poems about her mother's death—"The First Autumn" in this book and "After Four Years" in *In Time Like Air*—is tender and sorrowful. This death did not seem "right" or a fulfillment as did her father's. She has spoken of the "excruciating tensions set up by my mother's death from cancer," and the pain of this tension lingered for years.[4] In "The First Autumn" the poet addresses her mother, saying that

> in a little while
> You will be dead again
> After this first rehearsal
> Since then and all the pain . . .

and tries to take comfort in the idea that all of life "spends" itself. The October flowers, the falling leaves will soon be gone, but all of this is a "harvest" and not a grief. Her mother's delight in flowers has become a kind of living presence: "The garden speaks your name."

The sorrow is more intense in "After Four Years," where the poet grieves because she cannot "lay down" her mother's death and "let her go gently into the past." A lament in rhythmic, muted tones, each stanza uses a refrain that begins and ends it, and each approaches a possible way of laying down the "long burden" of sadness. It cannot be done in love, nor in solitude, nor in return to Europe ("the magical old trees and cities"); possibly it could

be done in prayer—but the poet has no "human prayer." Her
mother is pictured as "radiant," and, therefore, the grief is all the
more "unnatural," but it cannot be dispersed as in "The First
Autumn." This more moving poem is like a cry wrung from the
poet almost against her will.

Miss Sarton's feeling of belonging to two worlds—or to neither
—appears in poems that express either the sense of exile or a love
of the old world. "Homage to Flanders" tells of how, on her return
to Belgium with her parents when she was seven, she felt a sudden
rush of emotion at seeing "this low land under a huge sky that I
did not remember." [5] Some of the poems, like "Provence" and
"Return to Chartres," do not refer specifically to separation or
exile but set down the essence of a place long known. But the
more poignant ones dealing with Europe are those like "O Saisons! O Châteaux!" [6] In this poem a series of vivid, brief images
gives the impression of traveling rapidly, remembering each place
because it was associated with both love and parting; and the
mood of the whole is summed up in the line, "Across lost landscapes trains scream," which suggests the grief of the poet who is
forced to leave what she has so greatly loved. "Evening Journey"
pictures country scenes in France as glimpsed from a car that
passes rapidly through the villages and groves, down roads where
"animals and men were coming home." [7]

The conflict of loyalties between countries may be resolved,
Miss Sarton came to believe, by a realization of the universality of
the feeling of exile and of the need for human brotherhood.
"From All Our Journeys" begins, "I too have known the inward
disturbance of exile"; and the poem grapples with the sense of
being at home nowhere. [8] This feeling is not just a personal one, for
"The tears of men are all the tears of exile." The idea of knitting
together people and continents is deftly carried out by the use of
the sestina, and the poem ends with an image of a vast tree that
arches over all continents.

In 1940 Miss Sarton took an eight-month lecture tour of the
United States, visiting many small colleges. She has said of this
trip, "It was in a way my coming of age as an American. For I had
until then a very divided heart. . . ." [9] Her feeling of finally belonging in the United States is reflected not only in a series called
"American Landscapes" in *The Lion and the Rose* but also in the
fact that, after the publication of *The Land of Silence,* the theme

of exile is absent from her poems. There is, however, a sense that
the Old World is confronting the new in "Poet in Residence," [10]
a long free-verse poem in which she speaks in her own voice, for
it is based on her teaching during a summer session at Southern
Illinois University in Carbondale. The mood of this poem is
somber and at times bitter, as is seen in these typical lines:

> Heavy, heavy the summer and its gloom,
> The place, a place of learning, the difficult strange place,
> And for what reason and from how far did you come,
> To find the desolation and the thin soil,
> To find the great heat and the sudden rain,
> To listen for the long cry of the through train?
> · · ·
> The birds alone made welcome in the morning sun
> And all else strange. . . .

The reader of *Phoenix* is aware of how different this place of
learning is from Shady Hill School. The students in this university
seem never to have been awakened to the joy of study:

> You come to books as to a strange dull town
> Where you know no one by name and do not care,
> And never recognize the Waste Land as your own.

How, the poet asks herself, can a teacher communicate his "passion and belief"? She concludes that this is his task, difficult as it
is. "It takes a long time for words to become thought" and for
thought to be real and active in one's life. But this conclusion is
less interesting than the sense imagery of the poem, which catches
so memorably the atmosphere of summer in the Midwest—in such
lines as

> Lonely on the suffocating walks under the trees
> Where faces cross and re-cross bright with sweat,
> And damp hands clutch the books unmarked by love.
> · · ·
> Here in the center of America
> Steeped deep in the tiger-lily June
> Where the iced blue hydrangea
> Cuts the air like a tune,

Here where the parched bird is still at noon,
Here in the center of America where it is always noon . . .

In recent years Miss Sarton has bought an old house in New
Hampshire and has furnished it with some of the cherished pieces
brought from her home in Belgium. So she feels something of the
past around her, and several poems about the house show that she
has considered it a place of "calm arrival." [11] In 1967 Miss Sarton
collected a number of her country poems into a volume entitled
As Does New Hampshire, which she dedicated to her neighbors
in Nelson, her village, on its two-hundredth anniversary. All but
two of the poems in this book had appeared in earlier volumes,
but some of them may be mentioned because they show aspects
of her life today. They are arranged in a sequence of the seasons,
beginning with winter. During the deep snows of the New England winter, her house "creaks like a ship" with the "shifting
weight" of snow and icicles. The image of the ship is carried
throughout the four stanzas: during the day, it is "sailing out on
light"; at night, it anchors in "black-silver pools" of darkness; it
is like an ark, full of "scampering presences," creatures who leave
nuts about, or a "seed hoard"; and the very silence of the house
is intense like a gathering storm. In another winter poem, "A
Fugue of Wings," the sounds of various birds in the bare branches
intrigue the poet; her enjoyment of every bird in its individuality
is evident in the careful description of their movement and appearance: the jays "plummet down" and the chickadees "exalt/
Erratic line, rebound"; the nuthatch is "he of modest mien/ And
dangerous beak." The whole poem has an excited, fluttering
movement.

The poem "The Annealing" tells how she had settled down in
the house during the first year, feeling at home and at peace—
until the woodchucks began to devastate the garden. Getting rid
of them seemed a "hopeless war" until the neighbors came to help
her, and she realized the blessing of their presence:

Nothing more subtle; neighbors do not intrude.
Nothing more strong; their prescience toward
Whatever need is felt without a word—
We come now to exchange our solitude.

One particular neighbor, Perley Cole, is singled out in a poem entitled "A Recognition." He it is who has for years been "Pulling some order out of ragged land" surrounding her house. More than a hired man, he is a friend, respected because of his skill, "Holding the scythe so lightly and so true/ In slow sweeps and in lovely passes"; his genius, she thinks, is akin to a poet's, for both feel strongly about their work, and both bring order out of chaos.

"A Flower-Arranging Summer" shows the poet going out in the morning to gather flowers, wondering, "What can I bear to plunder?" and spending a long time, perhaps a whole morning, in the arranging—not wasting the time in this "long foolish flowery meditation" but being so absorbed that she feels then a part of eternity. One of the new poems in *As Does New Hampshire*, "A Guest," which has the precision, delicacy, and humor of some of her best work, plays with the idea that someone like herself, living so near the forest wilderness, is the intruder and stranger:

> My woods belong to woodcock and to deer;
> For them, it is an accident I'm here
>
> The young buck takes me in with a long glance
> And says that I, not he, am here by chance.

When a stranger knocks at her door, she is startled on opening it to see "an unfurry face," so completely does she feel a part of the place that she now considers home. And the tone of this poem, the identification that Miss Sarton feels with the animal world, is one familiar to readers of her other work, particularly a short prose book called *The Fur Person* (1956).

This book is described on the dust jacket as "the barely concealed true adventures of May Sarton's own cat." The story is told entirely from the point of view of the cat who, starting life as a stray "Cat About Town," eventually decides to settle down. He chooses as his "housekeepers" two kind ladies who become identified as "Gentle Voice" and "Gruff Voice," the latter of whom "sat for hours and hours in front of a typewriter, tapping out messages with her fingers" (63). The two ladies decide that, because of the cat's propensity for getting into fights and being badly mauled, Tom Jones (so named because he was a foundling) must be taken to the hospital and made into a Quaker cat. After this ordeal, he is changed from Terrible Jones to Gentle Jones, and he finds himself growing more and more fond of his housekeepers. When they move to a new house, he is upset, for one of his private "commandments" is "A Gentleman Cat Attaches Himself to Places Rather Than to People" (91). But having shown his indignation, he decides to remain with them anyway, and gradually he realizes that he has become more than a Gentleman Cat—he is, after some years, a Fur Person—"a cat whom human beings love in the right way, allowing him to keep his dignity, his reserve, and his freedom" (105). Since he is "truly loved by a human being" (106), he is content to remain with people for the remainder of his life. The whimsical tone of *The Fur Person* and the identification of the author with Tom Jones make it a distinctive animal story. Here are described briefly and perfectly the traits that every cat owner has noticed—the independent spirit, the guarded affection, the habits of solitude, and the wild joy in living.

The story of Miss Sarton's later life, including her buying and settling in the country house in New Hampshire, is told in *Plant Dreaming Deep*, published in 1967 as a sequel to *I Knew a Phoenix*. Here the autobiographical hints in the poems and in *The Fur Person* are explained and expanded. This book, like *The Fur Person*, is dedicated to "Judy," and the reader sees that Judy is "Gentle Voice," the friend with whom Miss Sarton lived for so many years in Cambridge. She is shown as someone who constantly encouraged Miss Sarton to try the "adventure" of moving to the new house, where she is now a frequent visitor.

The prologue of *Plant Dreaming Deep* sketches the twenty years of the author's life between the publication of her first book of poems (where she ended *Phoenix*) and her going to live in New Hampshire. She tells of the adventure of restoring the house that she found in the tiny village of Nelson—of knocking out a wall between two rooms, of adding windows and plumbing, of deciding on colors, and at last of moving in and arranging her belongings. Her first guest was Céline Limbosch from Belgium, a friend of many years, just the right person to help her bridge the gap between her ties with Europe and this new start in America. Later other visitors came, and she made friendships in the village, especially with Mildred and Albert Quigley, her neighbors.

But she had come to Nelson primarily to have a place of her own where she could be alone and write, so quite early in her life in the new house she established a routine of work from which she does not often depart. Much of the book tells of the mental and spiritual stocktaking that became possible in the "life-restoring silence" (29) of the house. She experienced not only solitude but loneliness; and gradually, as one season followed another, she came to see that her own inner person was changing—becoming more serene, less intense and anxious. She was beginning to integrate all the varied experiences of her earlier years and to feel that she had truly come home. The title of the book is taken from her own poem paraphrasing Du Bellay:

> Happy the man who can long roaming reap,
> Like old Ulysses when he shaped his course
> Homeward at last toward the native source,
> Seasoned and stretched to plant his dreaming deep.

Her life in the country is, she concludes, a "marriage of a wild natural world and an ethos brought here from Europe" (188). The tone of peaceful joy that runs through the book derives from her feeling that she at last is no longer an exile. On the day when Céline Limbosch came to the house, Miss Sarton says that they felt a wonderful fulfillment: "We had arrived through all the years, and the wars, and the deaths, through all the partings—when each time we thought we might never see each other again—through all the hopes and fears, to this moment of luminous quiet" (64).

And other guests have left reminders of themselves, weaving their "ghosts" into the fabric of the house. For example, whenever the hummingbirds return in the spring, it is a reminder of the visit of Basil de Selincourt, who was so delighted with them. It was he whose garden near Oxford contained shirley poppies, some of which now bloom in her garden at Nelson, another reminder of him. The garden itself means continuity with the past. Fritillaries remind her of Dorothy Wellesley, and the Chinese peonies bring back the picture of Ellery Sedgwick. Most of all, the garden holds memories of her mother, whose "light ghost is everywhere" in it (126).

The theme of continuity in the book is matched by an emphasis on the creation of order. The house stands near the village green, but behind it is a wilderness of brush and rough land, so that Miss Sarton's garden is "a small orderly pocket in a vast natural world" (123). She and Perley Cole together have "lifted the place out of its neglect and chaos into something like beauty and order" (114). The book is full of references to making space and to opening out. The big kitchen-living room made out of what had been two smaller rooms helped to answer her need for "air, light, and space" (33–34); and now the beauty of the house seems to make a constant demand for orderliness and lack of clutter. The very routine with which she orders her days is, she feels, a way of clearing space before her: "Routine is not a prison, but the way into freedom from time. The apparently measured time has immeasurable space within it, and in this it resembles music" (56–57).

The chief value of the house is shown as its being a perfect place for the writing of poetry. In her "freedom from time," she finds that her inner life becomes very intense; solitude "is a way of waiting for the inaudible and the invisible to make itself felt" (70), and from such solitude poetry can emerge. She has also found that the very problems of country life produce metaphors: gardening, like writing, asks much of the individual, but, in return it gives much; the experience of drilling for an artesian well taught her that "if one can go deep enough, one will come to rock" (151); Perley Cole's language is vivid and "pithy" like that of a poet, and he thinks of himself as a kind of "legendary figure who inhabits the center of a myth" (112).

All that she says about the writing of poetry makes clear that it cannot be separated from her growth as a person. In the first planning of alterations to the house, she saw it "as becoming my own creation within a traditional frame, in much the same way as a poet pours his vision of life into the traditional form of the sonnet" (34). The framework of the house, during her eight years in Nelson, has held a changing inner vision. The light, silence, and space that she planned for and achieved in the house suggest her need to absorb the experiences of her past, to come to terms with herself at the height of her career, and to understand more fully life's purpose.

At Nelson, Miss Sarton has had a chance to reflect and consider where she is going. Some of the "demons" she faced—and still faces, though they were especially prominent in her first winter in the house—concern her work as a *writer*. They are the demons of rage and self-doubt arising from disappointment at not having achieved great fame. Another demon takes the form of questioning the value of her poetry and novels, in comparison to other work she might have done, such as teaching under-privileged children. Alone in the house, she also faced the knowledge that time was getting short: she no longer had "an indefinite time ahead" (91). None of these tensions were entirely new; yet they stood out more sharply now that she was unprotected by family life and by routine social contacts. Always, during her years in the house, she has felt more "aware and intense" (94) than in other places.

If the house provides "the climate of poetry," that is also "the climate of anxiety" (60). But at the same time the house supports her and increases her "power to endure and to be renewed" (94). She finds that some of her attitudes are changing. She has learned, when kind neighbors helped her in many an emergency, that dependency is as much a virtue as self-reliance. She has also become aware of her changing attitude toward people: "The poet who had pored with passionate absorption over many a human face was, although she did not yet quite accept the fact, moving into a new phase. Just at dusk the hills that surround the village sometimes take the afterglow. They and the high church steeple are all lit up, making a luminous bowl in which the already shadowy village lies . . . a vision like this was subtly replacing in my attention the changing light on a human face" (93–94).

In the last chapter of *Plant Dreaming Deep,* she suggests that another change involves a kind of renunciation, which seems "the opening of a door into this new silence" (181)—the silence that is coming to mean more than "ambition and the world." She gives no more definite statement as to how she understands at present the purpose of life, but clearly she is moving towards a new phase.

In her work to date, to be discussed in the following pages, one of the persistent themes is that of the journey. It is interesting to see that in *Plant Dreaming Deep,* as well as in the poem "The House in Winter,"[12] she compares her house to a ship. She moved in on a rainy day in October; and, as she settled down to sleep after the strenuous day, she heard "the infinite number of sounds an old house contains in the night." They made her feel that she was on a ship, and "I did not know where the ship would take me, but I knew it was snug and beautiful, and I knew that its passenger was both inward and outward bound" (50). The reader of

Phoenix sees in this statement—and, indeed, in the whole tenor of the later autobiography—an indication of the eagerness and the energy with which Miss Sarton is moving outward toward the future, and inward toward a greater understanding of herself.

CHAPTER 2

The Heart Translated

I *Of Love*

IN *Encounter in April* (1937), Miss Sarton's first volume of poetry, three themes appear that are dominant in all her poetic works: love is a source of wonder and delight; love inevitably brings either parting or painful disillusionment; and art is more permanently satifying than life. Related to the last of these is what might be considered in this volume a minor theme—the desire for a perfection that is understood to be spiritual, intangible. This minor theme helps set apart the best poem in the book, a long narrative in free verse, entitled "She Shall Be Called Woman."

This poem may owe some of its power to the fact that it reminds the reader of William Blake's "Book of Thel," the tale that depicts a soul hesitant to be born into the flesh, or, in another interpretation, of a young girl reluctant to experience the physical aspect of sex. But "She Shall Be Called Woman" stands on its own as remarkable—especially for a young poet—in its simplicity and imaginative power. It tells the story of Eve from her creation to her acceptance of herself. She is pictured as at first lying passively "against the great curve/ of the earth"; she has just come to consciousness and does not want her body, or Adam's body on hers. Later, after intercourse with him, she feels desire; but she wants to deny it, hates it, and goes into the sea, hoping "to leave her body/ like a little garment," for she wants her soul, "the pure abstract," to exist without this painful encumbrance. But she finds no peace in denial of the body; instead, she begins to feel her self one with all other suffering bodies—she has no personal identity but is part of a great "wound" that means life. Then she at last falls into a healing sleep; and, when she awakens, she is suddenly aware of the mysterious wonder of her body, its beauty and complexity; now, paradoxically, "She would not ever be naked/ again," for she sees herself as having an outline:

The finite self
had gathered
and was born
out of the infinite,
was hers
and whole.

She now understands her purpose in the universe—to reproduce
her kind; her body is adapted to that end. She herself is "the
beginning,/ the never-ending,/ the perfect tree."

Of the other poems in the book, the most interesting are "First
Snow," which begins the volume, and the sonnets. "First Snow,"
with its heavily accented, three-beat line, has an almost hypnotic
rhythm like a mysterious incantation; it also has the flavor of a
haunting story from Grimm's fairy tales. It begins:

This is the first soft snow
That tiptoes up to your door
As you sit by the fire and sew,
That sifts through a crack in the floor
And covers your hair with hoar.

Throughout the four stanzas, in which every image increases the
feeling of an inevitable disaster, snow and whiteness, cold and
frost, are a metaphor for love so fierce that it freezes its victim
with despair; or, with a change of metaphor, the love is a hound
that somehow seems an embodiment of the cold and that "sav-
agely" attacks a deer. It is a "moon-blind/ Hound you will never
bind."

The sonnets, introduced by this fearful motif, deal with aspects
of love. A group of five at the beginning tells the story of a brief
affair that begins with a chance encounter—a meeting like that of
two deer in a wood "Startled and dazzled in each other's light."
The woman falls in love. The man, who is compared to a leopard,
"lithe and arrogant" with "clear eyes . . . gold as wine," does not
take the adventure seriously. It is all an "escapade," they part
gracefully, with no reproach from her, but she suffers. In the
group of fifteen sonnets near the end of the book, a narrative is
less apparent, but some again use animal imagery: the man is in
one compared to an antelope, wild and free; and the woman
hopes that love will steal upon him "warily" lest he take alarm and

think he is being forced to love against his will. In another sonnet, the lovers, when separated, hold spiritual communion; they are like birds, in that their minds can meet briefly in a mystical union, and "Then wheel, and each slide down the wind alone/ Back to his separate skin, his human feather." In Sonnet 13, lovers when reunited look into each other's eyes "As a faun looks at that sea-changed faun/ Reflected in a pool."

The most consistent theme in this group of fifteen sonnets is the difference between physical passion and real love. Passion involves only the flesh and therefore is not permanently satisfying. It is a tremendous force that in one poem has "grafted" the lovers "like two trees into one bark," but it has also wounded them and made them afraid of each other. This force is not love; rather, love is a separate entity, "luminous and wild,/ Lying between us like a sleeping child." In another sonnet, love is "the thing we'd never touched nor named/ But held between us like a crystal ball." And the speaker in a similar sonnet realizes that "the gentle flesh" is not enough to satisfy the soul's yearning, the essential loneliness of the individual, who dimly understands himself to be more than earth and "fervent blood."

The other poems in the book are divided into two groups, "Landscapes and Portraits" and "Fall of Petals," and the subjects are various: there are English landscapes, one depicting the warmth and contentment of an English summer; one on the formal perfection of Kew Gardens, where "the birds receive" and people look like choruses in an opera as they "compose themselves into the long perspectives of the trees." Of the portraits, several are inspired by paintings, such as "Portrait of the Artist," a word picture of Joos Van Cleve's self-portrait. The "fall of petals," in the second group, symbolizes the disintegration of a relationship, which brings a muted kind of sadness. In this grief, which is also touched upon in "Landscapes and Portraits," the poet finds comfort in reflecting about artists, like Keats and Mozart, who are not "among the living, the fallible, the beautiful destroyers" but show, through their art, a permanence that gives sustenance and rest for the disillusioned. In "For Keats and Mozart" the artists are seen as people who

> have created
> with human breath

> something outside of life, outside of death—
> the heart translated.

In general, these two groups of poems are decidedly inferior to the sonnets, "First Snow," and "She Shall Be Called Woman." The sonnets, even when they are, in the touch of self-pity, reminiscent of the worst of Elinor Wylie and Edna St. Vincent Millay, show competent workmanship. William Rose Benét's early comment about them, that they have "dignity and spiritedness," still is valid.[1] And, if one might tend to think that their quality depends on strictness of form, there is the excellence of "She Shall Be Called Woman" to show that Miss Sarton was capable, this early in her career, of writing distinguished free verse. But the other free verse poems are too diffuse; they are more like sketches for poems than finished products. Also, most of the poems in "Fall of Petals" are flawed by the constant reference to a blank, anonymous "you" who has no reality for the reader.

The poem "Request," however, deserves mention, not because it is remarkable in itself, but in one of its sentences it echoes something mentioned in the discussion of "She Shall Be Called Woman" —the idea that a body (here seen as words) can hinder the full development or understanding of soul. The speaker in the poem asks for silence instead of language,

> For silence reveals
> and words envelop
> in a pattern difficult to flavor
> with eternity.

This idea, of course, like Eve's wish for "the pure abstract," is at variance with valuing a work of art (a body) because it gives form to the intangible; but both ideas express a longing for a spiritual dimension to life.

II *The Heart Bereft*

Miss Sarton's next book of poetry, *Inner Landscape* (1939), emphasizes the painful aspect of love that had only been touched on earlier. Here the landscape of the speaker's interior life is a bleak one, symbolizing a heart bereft of comfort: there are wintry images—snow, barren fields, leaves falling. And yet, along with the desolation brought by unrequited love, there is a feeling of growth or achievement that arises from the pain. For the bleak landscapes indicate not only suffering but also an isolation that is, in the end, welcomed as necessary for writing the poems. The speaker in the poems is also an artist, who finds that tension and grief can be used. Basil de Selincourt, in a review of *Inner Landscape,* speaks of the "solemn dedication" to poetry that unifies the book—a dedication that "grounds the ultimate, creative personality on an ultimate renunciation, on an achieved independence, an impassioned solitariness." [2]

The sense of dedication is seen in the first three poems, "Prayer before Work," "Invocation," and "Architectural Image," all of which are concerned with poetry itself, its purity, precision, and perfection as compared to the warm, imperfect, diffuse passion that has been its origin. The speaker wishes to create something as lastingly beautiful as marble. In "Invocation" she asks that poetry "Be the abstraction, be the essence/ Inhuman, without hunger." And the architectural image she wishes to match with feeling is a spire, with its "soaring tension,—/ Flight, but deriving from the sternest line." Sternness is equated with the power of mind over emotion. Similarly, "Landscape" describes the process of creation. Here is pictured a dreamlike country where the earth reflects light from a dazzling sky; it is a "white earth changed as if by snow," and one feels that it is not real snow but rather the brightness of possibility—the chance for creation—for it is a wilderness of "infinite spaces." Such spaces are frighteningly unfamiliar at first, but the speaker expects to "Find at the end the simplest, the most lucid peace,/ Passion that takes a perfect form and stays inviolate."

Poems follow that tell the story of love not returned. The moods are as various as those of the grieving lover—now accusing, now lamenting, now gentle or tender, and again passionately demanding. In "Granted This World," the poet speaks to an "unbeliever" who has accused her of "making up" the whole affair—of imagining both her love and the response to it. The images are of a fantastic world of glass flowers, glass fruit, a whole orchard of glass trees; and, when the "unreal" fruit is picked and the glass shattered, there is a real wound on the wrist of the unbeliever and real blood flows. How could this be if it is all an imaginary state?

The love that may seem unreal because unexpressed can, nevertheless, cause acute pain to the lover and perhaps to others.

Many of the poems are sonnets in the Shakespearean form. In several, the beloved is referred to as "marble" because of the hardness and unresponsiveness of that material; but this hard quality—firmness, perfection—is what the speaker longs to instill into the poems. In the seventh and eighth sonnets a note of delight or pure joy suddenly appears: the experience of having loved, though hopelessly, lights the speaker's world; in a "blazing winter heaven" planets "swim a fiery pattern," and the enforced aloneness of the seemingly endless night makes her hear "thundering music in the emptiness." In the eighth sonnet, her passion is compared to a mounting wave, which, though it will inevitably break on "love implacable as stone," has in it a kind of delight.

In such sonnets the language is mostly conventional; but in the twelfth—the last of this series—a fresh, more interesting image appears, that of a field of nettles. The woebegone lover turns on herself with a touch of wry humor and to ask why she is distressed? She is in pursuit of a dream and finds herself "hemmed in with stinging weed"; and she still queries why she had expected that anything worth having would be obtained easily. The implication is that neither the course of love nor the writing of poetry is easy. Paradise, she tells herself, can never be peaceful: "Why now cry out against your stinging hand?/ This prickly country is that paradise."

In the remainder of the poems, grouped as "Summary," "Canticles," "Winter Landscape," and a final single poem called "Letter to James Stephens," the least good poems are similar, in their self-pity, to some of those in *Encounter in April*. But, for the most part, the change from the sonnet form contributes to fresher ideas and imagery, and some of the canticles with their fluid, open vowels sing with a delicacy and detachment that indicate a mastery of the grieving self. For example, the ear is pleased with lines like these from the first canticle:

> Behind what little mirror lies the country of your voice?
> What rivers the heart has seen but never the open eyes?
> What was your instrument, what rainy flute your choice,
> What lucid language, lighter than our human cries
> Did you once speak to call this voice your own?

Some of the themes in these last groups are similar to those already discussed. There are more wintry landscapes: "Transition" pictures someone walking in half-light through a waste of snow; and feeling is muted, all is stunned silence, indicating the aftermath of an emotional shock. "From a Train Window" and "Static Landscape" picture again a world "bitten with blight," terribly quiet, blank, and "bright with sterile snow." Usually the silence in such poems, as in the one beginning "The spirit comes back to silence like a dove," seems artificial; it is imposed from without on what would have been a warm turbulence—hence, the images of glass, ice, and unnatural brilliance. And the difference between passion and love is again noted, as in *Encounter in April*; for example, in Canticle 5, passion is like a restless wind, "banging," "tearing," seizing its victims and ravaging them. Love is more stable and solitary, not so filled with pain.

Another theme in the last groups, one related to that in the sonnet about the nettle field, is that the power of passion can be used to create the work of art. This theme is stated vigorously in the poem "Translation," where passion is compared to the clamor of bells within the lover. Passion can take a new course: "Bells, be translated!" And, in "The Memory of Swans," the lover considers how she might use passion for making something as beautiful, detached, and graceful as a swan. The most interesting of the poems that use this theme are two in which the idea is joined to still other pictures of cold, bleak landscapes. "Considerations" begins, "I am not native to this country" and then describes the quiet snowy wood that symbolizes detachment. The speaker concludes that

> Perhaps the perfect will
> Is in negation first when thinking seems to cease,
> When mind surveys a landscape absolutely still,
> And passionless observes the snow and the bough's strain
> As if not native to the earth,—aloof and foreign.

In "Map for Despair" the poet's necessary detachment is called "your island, created by yourself,/ Set in a space without horizon"; and she urges herself to accept and be glad of this "mental climate," this island she has won.

Throughout the book, there are frequent references to peace as something ardently desired but never to be had. The cold, quiescent scenes are immobile, not peaceful. In the last poem, "Letter to James Stephens," the poems are explained as being constructed "on the quicksand of despair" as a place where other people can find happiness:

> A house where every man may take his ease,
> May come to shelter from the outer air,
> A little house where he may find his peace.

Here again is the idea of using the painful emotion for the purpose of art.

III   Love and Art

The "double impulse" which Basil de Selincourt finds in the poems of *Inner Landscape* is that which unifies all of Miss Sarton's later poetry. It is "on the one side, the loving impulse to merge in passionate identification, on the other the creative impulse to hold aloof, that the moulding vision, the defining workmanship, may be perfected." [3] The two themes of love and art run, with varying emphases, through the four volumes of poetry published between 1948 and 1966, and they appear most clearly in the collected poems—*Cloud, Stone, Sun, Vine*—of 1961. The emotional power—the heart—is "translated" into the work of art. But in the later volumes—*The Land of Silence, In Time Like Air,* and *A Private Mythology*—there is increasing emphasis on the need to create not only art but character, so that the poet expands a theme of her first volume: the need for a spiritual quality in life.

The Lion and the Rose, which followed *Inner Landscape*, contains a memorable image in its first poem: "Vision is locked in stone." The lion, representing wildness, vision, or the creative power, is seen as a carving, as something still and defined. The idea that a vibrant force can, or must, be given shape or form runs through the whole book. In "The Lion and the Rose," the movement and "tawny fire" of the beast can only be kept in words (the stone) of the poem, after "The lion of the air is gone / With the great lion of the sun." Also, after all the bold, wild passion is gone, the rose of spiritual love may flower; the lion's departure seems essential if the softer magic of the rose is to appear.
There are three other poems in the first section of the book:

"Meditation in Sunlight" describes a mood of tranquillity induced by the light, space, and solitude of Santa Fe, New Mexico. A similar landscape in "Difficult Scene," though brilliantly sunny and apparently impersonal, seems to demand of the poet an austerity to match it—a renunciation of everything but purity of heart. The third one, "The Window," resumes the key theme of something boundless restricted within limits; the window frame outlines infinite spaces beyond it:

> The square explodes in space,
> The window opens into time—
> As poems breathe within their strict design,
> As holiness may look out from a face.

There follows a group called "American Landscapes," dealing chiefly with places in the South and in the West. Monticello is admired for its classic beauty, "this elegance, / This freedom in a form." But in "Charleston Plantations" and "Where the Peacock Cried" the materialism of the Old South and its traffic in slavery are the dominant themes. Decadent beauty is there, "savage as a peacock's scream, / Emblem of luxury and emptiness and death. . . ." Looking at a crucifix in Santos, New Mexico, the speaker marvels at the primitive urge for self-sacrifice and feels that, in contrast, modern man does not really love. "Indian Dances," which catches the rhythm of the dance in a manner reminiscent of Vachel Lindsay's "The Congo," develops the theme of controlled vision that is in this group of poems—as in all this volume. The speaker looks with awe at Boulder Dam, "A beauty sheer and clean and without error," and sees it as "Power in absolute control, freed as a gift, / A pure creative act."

In the next section, "The Work of Happiness," the title poem uses a tree, one of Miss Sarton's favorite images, as a symbol for happiness: it grows like a tree, "strikes its roots deep in the house alone," and is peaceful, serene. Other poems are about happiness in contemplation of the sensuous world. For example, "After a Train Journey" begins, "My eyes are full of rivers and trees to-night, / The clear waters sprung in the green"; and "In That Deep Wood" shows the mysterious fascination of a dark forest and the "People with green-drenched eyes" who might live there, immune from the distress of life. Other poems express happiness in the contemplation of particular lives, such as that of the white-haired man who "sowed faith wherever he moved; his was a "Love not transcending the person but incarnate / As in his own hand given you in greeting."

Happiness derived from the creation of poetry is the theme of "New Year Wishes"; and "Definition" attempts to describe just what the creative process is. The short, three-beat lines of this poem state succinctly the key idea of the book: that feeling and imagination must be held within form. Its concern that "You strange airy lovers / Imagination-driven" be "held in the stern net / Difficult mind-woven" reminds the reader again of the vision of the lion "locked in stone."

Throughout *The Lion and the Rose,* one is made aware that happiness is associated with peace and simple living that is close to the earth; it is not passion or vision. It is not (as shown in "Now Voyager") something that a poet can ever really have. In a long poem, "My Sisters, O My Sisters," Miss Sarton explores the relationship between a poet and a woman and wonders if one can ever successsfully be both creator and lover. Was Emily Dickinson a good poet because she "renounced" and so learned "to fuse emotion /With thought"? Eve and Mary are seen to be "our stem," and they represent passion and wisdom; but is it possible to be both of them? A woman must learn the skill to do so, "To be Eve, the giver of knowledge, the lover; / To be Mary, the shield, the healer and the mother."

In the section "Love Poems," a few express the delight and wonder of being in love; and some take up themes of *Inner Land-scapes*—loss, renunciation, or the pain of loving. One of the most graceful and delicate of the lyrics, "The Lady and the Unicorn," is reminiscent of "Granted This World" in that again there is an imaginary quality about this love not brought to fruition. The poet speaks of himself as the unicorn bowing before the lady; both are woven into the tapestry and "into history" yet poignantly unreal and strange as the pictured scene: "Know we are woven all in mystery / The wound imagined where no one has bled. . . ." Passion, which inevitably brings pain, is described in another poem, "Magnet," with images of heaviness, "the weight unbear-able." In the third of "Three Sonnets" the violence of mutual passion is expressed in words like "bruises," "jar," and "hurled";

the sonnet ends with this striking image of the two lovers cut off from the world by their own painful emotion:

> The tension grows. The circle narrows down,
> Until it is two pairs of haunted eyes:
> By love bound, by love wounded, still we stand
> Like two Sebastians, pierced, and hand in hand.

A parallel poem to "Definition," mentioned above, is "Definition of Love" in which the poet attempts, through short, spare lines, to express the bare essence of love as the core of life. It begins: "Not so much terrible as pure, / So pure it is nothing. It is alone." And the poem compares love to the "round" note of music; to an almond stone, stripped down; to the "nerve of the leaf"; and to "the attar of being." Neither of the poems of definition quite succeeds, perhaps because each is rather self-conscious, prosy, and lacks such a vivid image as the lion, "vision locked in stone." But one of the most successful of the love poems, "O Saisons! O Châteaux!" combines the idea of lost love with that of being torn between loyalty to the old and new worlds; it also, in its refrain, "We only keep what we lose," touches again on the idea of necessary renunciation.

In the last group of poems, "To the Living," there are a few occasional poems—such as one of bitter regret and indignation at the loss of great trees in the New England hurricane of 1938 and another about the killing of Negroes in Detroit in 1943. Others express bewilderment and protest at war—"Navigator" and "Unlucky Soldier" both lament the need for youthful strength and gaiety to be changed or chaneled for the purpose of destruction. The poet sees both Chartres and Flanders in the light of the tragedy of war. In most of the poems of this section, the individual's responsibility for world conflict and chaos is stressed: "I, the plain citizen, have grown disorder / In my world" says the narrator, whose indifference has led to the Negroes' death. The work of the living, the reader is told, should be to *care,* to have active concern about all suffering; and feeling strongly is praised as the opposite of indifference.

The living should also, the poet believes, train and cherish the imagination. In "These Pure Arches" imagination is the power that creates not only art but also love and peace in the world. A similar idea is stated at more length in the four-part poem, "To the Living," in which "The need to kill what is unknown and strange" can only be overcome by seeing, through imagination, the whole world as home and all men—the refugees, beggars, strangers—as bound together by strong human ties. In this poem the theme of exile, which is personal in the love poems, becomes universal; for who, the speaker asks, has not known both flight and loneliness?

> Each is an exile from the whole. The agony
> Of separation is the human agony.
> From the four corners of the earth
> How bring us home into humanity?

Those who make the attempt to "bring us home" are considered creators in the last poem, entitled "Celebrations." The poet creates his work of art, but all who show love and concern—and thus widen mental and emotional horizons—help to create a better world. These are all those who "Profess belief, move from faith, act to plan, set chaos in a fiery glass / Where the future can be seen, organic, healthy as a plant. . . ." "Celebrations," which is in free verse and which is too directly stated to have the impact of a more subtle poem like "These Pure Arches," does summarize in the phrase "set chaos in a fiery glass" the theme of *The Lion and the Rose:* that compelling force—love, vision, wildness—can be ordered and made tangible in both art and life.

In Miss Sarton's next book of poetry, *The Land of Silence* (1953), the title poem and the "Letter to an Indian Friend" which follows it suggest that the basic image for this volume may have been derived from visits to New Mexico. As in *The Lion and the Rose,* the poet is fascinated by the utterly quiet, bare landscape with its mountains and sunshine, where time either ceases to matter or seems in some way identical with space. The scene is not peaceful in the usual sense of that word; rather, it is an intense, vibrant stillness out of which may come creation—either a poem or a new freedom—and a certainty as to one's purpose and destiny. The land of silence might be compared to what Charles Morgan has called the "creative pause"; or it resembles somewhat the active passiveness of the saints, a waiting that is selfless and serene—contemplation that is the point toward which all action moves.

The silence is described in the title poem, "The Land of Silence," as both a power and a place. As a healing power, the imperceptible passing of time brings relief after an emotional shock: "Death is so close to life that we can bear it. / The smallest veins drink time and breathe again." Then, silence as a place is where mountains rise up in the distance and a dove moves about in the bare trees of the foreground; all is quiet, but the hills and "The intense violet light" suggest active involvement, just as the dove symbolizes a peace that might eventually come. Bare as the scene is, it is not passive, for "This is the land of bones and violent dreaming." The poem ends with a couplet showing the land of silence as a place to be sought for and attained only with effort: "Even more than love we search for faith / Who in this high air must gasp for breath."

In "Letter to an Indian Friend," the speaker asks Tilano, the old Indian, how to take "the first step" toward "A land of work and silence, a whole land"; and the emphasis is on attaining the land through renunciation and religious faith. In "Because What I Want Most Is Permanence" poetry and prayer are seen as the same force, which "makes the whole world both intense and still"; therefore, the speaker resolves to renounce passion for the sake of creating such a world. An examination of these three poems in sequence shows the meaning of "death" in the first one: it is the painful surrender of self that is necessary for growth in either poetry or life.

In subject matter, the poems in this book resemble those of previous volumes: there are landscapes and nature poems, poems on love, on friendship, on death, on the need for brotherhood in the world. But in all of these groups, the land of silence is referred to, directly or obliquely, so often as to give unity to the whole. Some poems, as already indicated, deal with the creation of poetry. The simplest of these, "Journey toward Poetry," received the Reynolds Lyric Award of the Poetry Society of America in 1952. In it, the bewildering multitude of possible images that flash into the poet's mind are tossed at the reader in the first stanza in lines that use repetition and consonance to give a fine rushing movement comparable to the "mad exploration" going on in the poet's mind.

In this first stage of excitement, the poet feels

shot out across foreign borders
To visionary and abrupt disorders.
The hills unwind and wind up on a spool;
Rivers leap out of their beds and run. . . .

Then, in the second stanza, "composed imagination" chooses, as if inevitably, the right image. The poet is now certain, and the movement of the lines is slowed with heavy accents:

To be still, to be silent, to stand by a window
Where time not motion changes light to shadow
Is to be present at the birth of creation.

Here again is the land of silence. It is also referred to, in connection with poetry, in the second part of "Two Songs," where the speaker, who has been wounded by life, turns for consolation to art; the "myth" or "invented" love has permanence in the silent words of the poem:

Only the myth held in the mind,
Only the myth held in the word
Resists, resists the whole real world,
Untouched, untouchable as stone,
And silence blesses it, is kind.

Several poems present extended images that express the poet's longing for a perfect union of form and content—the powerful "vision" (as in "The Lion and the Rose") that will be shaped with the strict outline needed for permanence and yet allow the vision to go on expanding in the mind of the reader. One such image is a group of trees ("The Sacred Wood"—sacred because the inspiration of the artist is akin to a religious experience); they are tall, straight trees that look like columns of a temple. They "define the empty air" and remain immovable through all the changing life of the seasons. Similarly, a stream is used as an image for the poem—moving, alive, yet held within its banks ("At the Bottom of the Green Field She Lies"); and in "Boy by the Waterfall" the poet catches a brief glimpse of a boy diving into a pool in "the dappled green light" and for a moment sees him as the perfect embodiment of a dream.

The landscapes and interior scenes are various. Some are not symbolic of the poet's inner life or of the creative process; they are pictures presented for pure delight. Such are the description of a Christmas tree ("The Tree") and "Summer Music," in which alliteration and assonance show the "green air" and "green sound" of lawns, pastures, and hedges. Others refer obliquely to the problem of form and content, though in them, too, the picture itself is central. In "The Swans," the controlled, beautiful movement of two swans—their passion expressed with grace—entrances the speaker. "Villanelle for Fireworks" says that some vibrant beauty cannot be captured in art—"We cannot give the falling star a home"—yet this poem tries to do so in its intricate rhyme and brilliant images. Some poems, such as "Transition" and "Winter Grace," both poems about autumn, are scenes setting forth the speaker's grief or anxiety. "In a Dry Land," picturing the relief brought by rain after long drought, also gives an image for a disrupted relationship that is healed.

Several poems deal with the need for brotherhood. In "Take Anguish for Companion," a sharing, through imagination, of the suffering of all men, an understanding that each is responsible for the world's pain, means accepting anguish and finding that doing so creates energy and joy. This idea is made memorable by a very concrete picture of abstract "man" who is first seen as "always at our side, starving and weeping, / Curved like a mother over his misery, / Huge and abandoned like a giant sleeping. . . ." If man, however, finds himself not alone, those who have shared his grief see him transformed:

> He is suddenly willing joy instead of power,
> Shaken to the marrow by joy as by a flame,
> Bending with mad delight toward a flower,
> Secret and tender, violent, he came
> Up from the darkness toward his haunting name.

A poem quite different in tone, which yet has concern for all suffering as its theme, is "The Caged Bird," where the bird that hurls itself wildly against the bars at night seems a symbol of all struggles against vast, impersonal forces.

Of the love poems in this book, "Leaves before the Wind" sets forth the theme used in previous volumes: that passion leads to despair. In this poem the individual is seen as helpless before the wind of passion, "this flowing fire," because he knows that "there are no roots," and only despair can be the outcome. Another poem uses wind in a quite different way. "Kinds of Wind" begins with lines in which onomatopoeia, alliteration, and assonance give the sound of wind in wheat and barley fields. Then a "fiercer blast" symbolizes passion that is painful but can "break through" to a place of detachment, like cold blue sky behind the clouds. The detachment seems identified with the land of silence, which is "pure love"; for "the wind's heart is still. . . ." A similar idea is found in "Evening Music," in which the land of silence is reached in love that is called "a point of burning far from passion."

A series of eleven love sonnets, entitled "These Images Remain," uses the two themes just mentioned—that passion contains intense joy but is "close to grief" and that renunciation or parting can lead to real love, which is silent and peaceful and brings forth new imaginative power. But in Sonnet 4, which gives to the rose the familiar sexual connotations, it is the fulfillment of passion—not its renunciation—that leads to the power of the land of silence. After the petals have all opened, they "Rest on the air in silent consummation"; the rose, now "immense and quiet," is "like the saint detached from its own fall." As in "The Lion and the Rose," spiritual peace and power come after the end of passion. Sonnet 10, which perhaps gives the best expression to the main ideas of the sequence, shows the relation between love and the land of silence. Its tone is serene and confident. It begins,

> These images remain, these classic landscapes
> That lie, immense and quiet, behind eyes
> Enlarged by love to think only in shapes
> That compass time and frame the changing skies . . .

Though the passion must eventually end—either by death, for "we are caught by time," or by separation—the new power of seeing what love has brought remains as a series of remembered pictures. A permanence has been attained through imagination.

The last poem in the book, "Now I Become Myself," has, like the sonnet just mentioned, a sense of achievement after long struggle. Here the exhilarating realization is that one need not rush madly hither and yon, for the land of silence is outside time. It is the place of creation that is reached by love, by being "always spent"; and, in the light of the whole book, this love can be seen either as a personal attachment or as a love of mankind.

IV *Philosophical Poetry*

In Time Like Air (1958) was the next of Miss Sarton's volumes of poetry. Unlike the previous books, this one contains no poems of social concern and only two—"Where Dream Begins" and "Lifting Stone"—that deal specifically with the writing of poetry. There are three that can be considered chiefly nature poems: "Green Song" is reminiscent of other poems praising the bright air and delicate sounds of summer; "Mediterranean" pictures the ancient, peaceful landscape of Europe; and the best of the three, "The Olive Grove," is such a fine matching of sound and sense, each word adding to the idyllic peace and lightness of the scene, that one can see why one reviewer has called Miss Sarton "perhaps above all a limner." [4] Reading the first two stanzes of this poem, one is aware of the subtle music of the *o* and *e* sounds:

> Here in the olive grove,
> Under the cobalt dome,
> The ancient spirits move
> And light comes home,
>
> And nests in silvery leaves.
> It makes each branch a cloud,
> And comes and goes, and weaves
> Aerial song aloud.

But most of the poems in this book are philosophical rather than descriptive. They are thoughtful and meditative without being heavily didactic, as are some of Miss Sarton's earlier poems. She is now beginning to achieve the blending of thought and passion to which she had long aspired. The title poem of the volume, written in the tradition of the seventeenth-century Metaphysical poets, is, in the words of Robert Hazel, "an expertly accreted analogy, both literally and figuratively crystalline. . . ." [5] Here the problem set by the speaker is how one can be selfless and yet have an identity, a self. Or how, to use the words of an earlier poem, can compassion and passion be the same or exist in the same place? If water dissolves salt, causing it to lose its identity, which is later regained in the air, then, "What element dissolves the soul / So it may be both found and lost, / In what suspended as a whole?"

The answer is given: love makes for selflessness—it is comparable to water—but only time can be the "air" for a person. The "first intense attachment" must precede the slow growth of the "faultless crystal of detachment" that is the ideal. Essentially, the problem presented in this poem is similar to that of Miss Sarton's first published poem of real excellence, "She Shall Be Called Woman"—how can a human being endure to be both body and soul, with their conflicting demands? An interesting feature of both poems is the calm objectivity with which such a burning question is set forth—an objectivity achieved in the earlier poem by narrative form and in the later by metaphysical "argument."

The desire for balance or poise runs through the book. There are the opposed claims of emotion and mind; can they be reconciled? Such is the theme of "Dialogue," a humorous treatment of reason versus passion, in which the "teacher of logic" argues with the poet. A poem called "Song" mocks the idea that man can be only mind; such a condition is as impossible as that gravitation can be suspended and "The juggler on his wire / Leap with pure lightness / And never fall to yearning. . . ." A much more distinguished poem, "Somersault," again uses the image of the tightrope walker, who is able to balance all tension: he "masters his own loss" and "springs from heaviness." There are many images of weight—words like "densities," "burdens," and "stumbling" suggest the full complexity of adult life; and the tightrope walker symbolizes a longed-for resolution of conflict. In "Reflections in a Double Mirror," the anxiety of an individual expressed in the first stanza is paralleled—"reflected" line by line or couplet by couplet—in the second stanza by a feeling of reassurance. Firmness and blessing are just as "real" as the anxious dreams of being lost in a wood or in "the bog, indifference, dragging quicksand."

One of the conflicts of the thoughtful person is between the world and the individual self. "The Frog, That Naked Creature" sets forth the dilemma of someone who feels too strongly and therefore seems either ridiculous or an object of pity. How can such a person grow a protective covering—or *should* he? Would he then be "mature"? A more familiar conflict, appearing in earlier volumes, is between physical passion and real love; but now the need for balance is more strongly emphasized. The sonnet "The Light Years" compares lovers to constellations; their briefly perfect love, which can "reverse the elements, / And bring down to the earth the starry sky," is a delicate, tense balance. And another poem that uses images of feathery lightness is "Spring Day," in which the lovers "At last . . . inhabit the dream, are really floating" because the perfection of the clear, bright day has brought their feeling into a temporary peace.

Most of the love poems in this volume—except for a few like "By Moonlight" and "Lady with a Falcon," which have the despair and cruelty of love as themes—refer either to the dual nature of love or to its power to bring about a wholeness of personality that harmonizes the jangling confusion of the world. In "The Return," love is both the "bright dry mind" and the cloud or wind of passion. "The Action of the Beautiful" describes the loved person's beauty as so powerful that "It fuses consciousness to a new balance. . . ." A similar balance is seen in "On Being Given Time," where a timeless peace (like the land of silence) can be achieved by means of love; in this realm, time seems to expand "like the long ripple that opens out beyond / The duck as he swims down the tranquil pond. . . ."

The tone of achieved peace is also in "The Metaphysical Garden," which, although in free verse, gives an impression of strict form because of the meticulous diction; no word or phrase could be omitted and none could be exchanged for another. The poem, another extended analogy, says that exploring a relationship with a lover is like walking slowly through an "amazing garden, hidden in the city, / Tranquil and complicated as an open hand." The speaker is addressing his lover and recalling their visit to that garden. The mood is one of wonder and suspense, yet an overwhelming feeling of security is as much a marvel as what they see and hear—the "dappled loggias," the "Diapason of faintly stirring leaves," and a cardinal that "flashed through the willow / And suddenly screamed." These lines in the second part of the poem approach a direct statement of the theme:

> And here it seemed we were part of a discourse
> On the ancient themes,
> Perspective and enclosure,
> Desire raised and fulfilled
> To this complex alive composure.

The perfection of the garden and its mystery reflect those qualities in the love of the two people. They enjoy all the intricacy of
the relationship—the climbing "lightly" up to an "intense enclosure" and the descent afterward to the slopes, down to "contemplation" and the "unbroken sunlit peace of knowing."

The need for balance is also recognized in poems that deal
with the conflict between body and soul. Such is the one beginning "These were her nightly journeys made alone," which
describes a woman's subconscious "burdens" that she can ignore
during the day but is subject to in sleep. Then she falls into
"heaviness"—perhaps of remorse, fear, or hopelessness—some kind
of hell in an "Imprisoned plunge / Sucked by dense air; / Or
worse, vertiginous oceans with no floor." But one night she is
aware of "some angelic power" which makes it possible for her to
"Reverse the motion, plunge into upwardness"; and, from then
on, she struggles, in the daytime, to retain this "thrust of hope"
which is her growing awareness of soul. Now, even in the night-
mare descent to heaviness, she is able to remember the other
aspect of her being and feel herself "both grounded and in flight."

Another interesting treatment of duality is in "To the North,"
where the contrast is between the richness, passion, and decay of
the South ("The purple seas under a mountain shadow, / The
rich and crumbling ruins in the hills. . . .") and the self-control
and self-knowledge symbolized by the "cold North."

What is suggested in most of these poems that emphasize balance is, as in Miss Sarton's first volume, the desire for a spiritual
dimension in life—a desire implicit in "In Time Like Air," with its
question about how one can be selfless. It runs through a poem
that gives an imaginative picture of Rainer Maria Rilke's mystical experience ("At Muzot"), which made him aware of body's
not conflicting with spirit but being identical with it. Coming to
such an awareness is a "journey" that is both "infinite" and "immobile."

In a similar vein are two specifically religious poems, "Nativity" and "Annunciation," both based on Renaissance paintings.
The first one begins:

> O cruel cloudless space,
> And pale bare ground where the poor infant lies!
> Why do we feel restored

As in a sacramental place?
Here Mystery is artifice,
And here a vision of such peace is stored,
Healing flows from it through our eyes.

"Mystery is artifice" is the key line to the poem; the formality and "geometric" arrangement of the picture somehow release power. The statuesque quality of the figures suggests to the speaker an inward joy and praise quite unlike human emotion. In "Annunciation," too, it is "perspective" that "leads us on / From matter and from moment"; the strictness of "converging lines" draws the spectator away from the material to the spiritual world.

With a similar theme but a completely different tone is "The Phoenix," a poem about the mythical bird that "must consume himself to be reborn." As a symbol of the urge toward the spiritual life, he can become an annoyance when he is not needed; the poem begins with a tone of exasperation:

It is time the big bird with the angry neck
We have cajoled and cursed
Went home to die, or whatever he must do
When his heart would burst.

His "lost cry" and his "cold and jewelled eyes" are a constant reproach to the speaker, who softens in the end to ask if perhaps "we ourselves" are to blame, we "who drove an angel from us / Because our hearts were torn?"

The poems of *In Time Like Air* are, on the whole, more carefully and intricately designed than those of the earlier books. It is as if greater depth of thought and weight of emotion find their truest expression in strict form. For example, the elegy "All Souls" joins the intensity of grief and music that comes from skillful use of repetition and echoing sounds; the "cold bleak voices" of the birds on a winter morning saying "Remember and forget, forget, remember" blend with the "lost human voices" that echo in the speaker's mind; and the whole poem is a complex interweaving of love, mourning, and memory. Of the other poems on death, those on Miss Sarton's father and mother have been mentioned elsewhere; they, too, are among her best. They, too, have regularity of meter and rhyme. Even the six translations from French poetry which appear at the end of the volume are in regular form. It is as if the poet has found such intense delight in the creation of poetry that she no longer needs to speak of it so much—as in the earlier books—and as if no subject is too abstract or too painful to be shaped into memorable form.

V Journey for Significance

In 1961 Miss Sarton published a volume of poems selected from four previous books, all of them except *Encounter in April*. She called this volume *Cloud, Stone, Sun, Vine*, from the lines in her poem "At Muzot":

> Angels, often invoked, become a fact.
> And they have names, Cloud, Stone, Sun, Vine,
> But the names are interchangeable.

The title suggests the author's preference for imagery from landscape; and, in its context, it reminds the reader of her concern with the conflict or harmony of body and soul. The book contained not only the selected poems but some new ones—several (discussed in Chapter 1) about Miss Sarton's house in New Hampshire, and a series of twenty sonnets.

The selected poems are arranged, not chronologically, but according to themes, giving the reader a chance to review those discussed in the earlier volumes. Under "American Places" and "O Saisons! O Châteaux!" are the poems about the New World and the Old, travel between them, and the feeling of exile resulting from being at home in neither. A section called "The Sacred Wood" contains poems about the writing of poetry. Two sections contain love poems: "The Action of the Beautiful" deals with love as peace and tranquil beauty; and "Leaves before the Wind" contains chiefly poems on love as passion and energy. In "Binding the Dragon" are poems on the problem of intense feeling and emotional balance. Those on death and religious aspiration are grouped under "All Souls"; and the last section, "To the Living," is devoted to poems of social concern.

Miss Sarton's next book of poetry, *A Private Mythology* (1966), continues and amplifies an idea touched on in the earliest volumes and made more specific in *In Time Like Air*—the search for spiritual peace. It is a book about a journey that is both outer and inner in meaning.

The first section of the book deals with Japan, India, and Greece. Here the poet's concern is not merely to describe places and people but to understand them. In an inn at Kyoto, the speaker realizes that she inhabits "a marvelous world / Where every sense is taught / New ways of perceiving." And the seeing which begins as a "camera eye," an outside view, becomes seeing from the inside. In Japan, the change from outer to inner comes in the poem "An Exchange of Gifts," where a tired, middle-aged servant brings the tourist a gift of a fan in appreciation of something given to *her*. The generosity of the servant and her unexpected smile, says the speaker, "Broke the pane of glass / Between me and all things: / I am inside the landscape." In India, another human contact brings a sense of understanding, not just seeing and recording. When the narrator slips and falls in the dust, and the people who had been so "unsmiling" immediately gather around to help, it is "Worth a scraped knee / To land on this earth at last, / To be helped alive. . . ."

The poems about Japan are full of delicate imagery—of paper walls, mists, "translucent flowers" and "That feathery elegance, bamboo." The series "Japanese Prints" contains a number of short poems in short lines, suggesting tenuous outlines and austere beauty. The quiet humor of the Japanese is also caught in poems like "Tourist," which reads:

> Boa constrictor
> Who has swallowed
> Too many temples!

"The Stone Garden" describes a place of such absolute simplicity —fifteen rocks artfully arranged on bare sand—that any slight change about it, such as a falling leaf or a shaft of sunlight, gives variation; and the bold austerity of the place stimulates the mind.

The poet's first impression of India is of "an impenetrable world," where everything is "too thick, too many." Most of the poems about India contain images of this multitudinous world and of heavy, slow motion. All of them, one reviewer says, "have the power of outcry"; he feels that Miss Sarton's indignation and surprise at what she saw give a "new range" to her poetry.[6] One of the best poems, "The Great Plain of India Seen from the Air," supports this view; it has the power that comes from an immense wonder, a dislike mixed with awe. It contrasts the "bright snow"

of the mountains that seem like "distant gods" with the earth
that is so far removed from anything vital or godlike. The dust
that endlessly settles over the arid plain seems a symbol of the
terrible lethargy and hopelessness of India—a will to live in the
past that makes the present barren of energy. But there is a similar awe, without the distaste, in the poem "The Sleeping God,"
or Vishnu; for the picture is of a "Young man relaxed in beauty,"
asleep and "vulnerable" yet immensely powerful. The paradox is
of the godlike love made possible because the god is both beyond
pain and humanly involved in it.

Going from India to Greece, the poet enters a bright, more
familiar world where the "knife-clean air" is almost "too brilliant"; for, after the "dark / Edgeless and melting" of India, "Who
can bear this shining? / The pitiless clarity?" There is a poem
about Mycenae, where the "death-haunted" past and the rural
present are equally real; and there is one that captures the echoing mystery of Delphi, with its fierce crags and "Eagles floating /
On high streamers of wind." Both Poseidon and Athene are presences at Lindos, where the horizontal line of the "flat sea / As
blue as lapis" contrasts with the images of height, the "arduous
stairways" up to the "roofless temple" of Athene. In the midst of
this lightness and clarity, the poem "Nostalgia for India" shows
the power of strange, irrational forces; for the traveler in a clean,
"unmysterious" hotel room in Athens feels a sudden longing for

> my dark cell
> In Orissa
> Where I was visited
> By a white lizard
> With emerald eyes,
> By an articulate frog,
> And sometimes, very late,
> By a wandering shrew.

Perhaps the most interesting of the Greek poems is "Birthday
on the Acropolis," which suggests the unifying threads of the
whole book. Here the reader especially feels that the journey is
not only a physical one involving the outer world but also a
a search for significance in personal life. The search requires that
some kind of a whole be made of the shimmering bits of experience, all of one's private world of the past; and it implies that a

middle-aged person can realize he has long been seeking some kind of rebirth. Miss Sarton, who speaks in her own person in this poem, remembers how the goddess Athene had "towered" over her childhood, suggesting an answer or an "opening" of a mystery. Now, on her fiftieth birthday, the poet feels that she is at a "primary place"—the Acropolis represents the heights of both the natural and the supernatural; here she might achieve an understanding that is poise, "So that all clarity / May meet all mystery / As on the spear's point." Here also she is confronted by "the archaic smile," which is "beyond suffering," suggesting a supernatural way to meet the pain of life.

Not only this poem but others throughout the book suggest that the answer sought by suffering humanity is to be found in a comprehensive love in the world, which might be the love of God. This idea is conveyed in a much more subtle manner than in the early rhetorical and didactic poems. Here, it informs the delicate humor at the expense of both tourists and guides; and it is shown in an all-pervasive warmth of tone, a love of every leaf, animal, and god as well as every person. In Japan, paper walls "Slide open / To bring those ancient members of the family, / Twelve plum trees, / Into the house. . . ." And other beings are mentioned with tenderness: "A kingfisher, intent / His long bill water-bent"; the worshipers in India who bathe in the sacred river; and the Greek grandmother who "Calls out greetings / And swears loudly from her bed."

The love of creation is akin, in the poems, to a desire for openness. Only when one remains open, unprotected, willing to be changed or hurt, can he achieve full stature as a human being. This idea is not new in Miss Sarton's writing, but it is especially noticeable in this book without ever being directly stated. Where in an earlier poem she writes, "Not ripeness, but the suffering change is all," [7] in *A Private Mythology* she says a similar thing by means of images of delicacy, openness, and translucence—the blossoms of Japan, the mists, and paper umbrellas; the Greek temples, where the spaces between the pillars are "open as justice," and one sees the "world-opening sea." In India, the god Vishnu is "flower-fragile, open to the least"; and for that reason he is powerful. Conversely, a lack of openness is a kind of death, as in the poem about Lazarus, suggested by the Anglo-Saxon sculpture in Chichester Cathedral. Here Lazarus, brought back

from the grave, "relearns despair" as he looks at the so-called
living people, gazes "Upon us, men carved out of sleep / Who
wish to pray but have no prayer."

The Lazarus poem provides a link between the first and second
parts of the book. Part II, which deals with America, the world
to which the "weightless traveler" returns, contains poems about
the New England countryside, about animals, and about people
(in the final series entitled "Elegies and Celebrations," where
particular people are praised). Again, as in the first half of the
book, the love of creation and the desire for openness appear as
themes. But true openness is not softness; it implies a hard
boundary containing it. "Of Havens" presents the ideal of a
human being who is always available to others, "An ever-welcom-
ing self that is not fenced"; but such an ideal is impossible (man
is not God)—"The unsheltered cannot shelter," and walls are
necessary. Similarly, "An Observation" begins "True gardeners
cannot bear a glove"; and the poem suggests that hands which
move sensitively among tender roots inevitably grow scarred.
Love is not always gentle; it must sometimes be "rigorous" or
"hard" in order to "stay sensitive." A quiet poem called "Still Life
in Snowstorm" presents the picture of richness and beauty
framed or contained within a boundary, and in the last stanza the
line "No drop of it can spill" recalls by its very difference the line
of the Twenty-third Psalm, "My cup runneth over."

The idea of rebirth, stated in the Lazarus poem and implicit in
many others in this volume, is in the New England poems,
"Learning about Water" and "Artesian Well"; and it is touched
on differently in one of the animal poems, "A Village Tale," the
story of a woman who, in a fit of willful madness, drowned one
of her dogs in the horse trough and buried him in the garden.
The other dog, as soon as she had gone, dug him up and found
him not quite dead. When the woman returns home, both dogs
sit waiting. The poet wonders how she could face the truth—
"Two wagging tails, four bright eyes shifting"; for "She could
face murder. Could she face redeeming?" Nobody knows:

> All that the village sees is that the dog
> Sits apart now, untouchable and sacred,
> Lazarus among dogs, whose loving eyes
> Follow her back and forth until she dies.

VI *Politics and Religion*

The title of Miss Sarton's latest book of poetry, *A Grain of Mustard Seed* (1971), refers to Christ's words to his disciples, "Have faith as a grain of mustard seed"; and the dominant idea of the volume is the implied question, How can one have faith when the world is torn by violence and bowed under suffering? The chief poems in the book concern politics and religion; they express, more urgently than the author has done before, both pain and a seeking for answers to difficult problems.

In Part I, poems on racism and violence in America speak harshly of the poet's bitterness and impatience with wrong. "Easter, 1968" is a moving lament for the death of Martin Luther King; and " 'We'll to the Woods No More, the Laurels Are Cut Down' " concerns the killing of students at Kent State University. In other poems there is an attempt to understand murderous impulses, both in oneself and in the world. A five-part poem, "Invocation to Kali," is filled with images of pain, for Kali is the Oriental goddess of violence and destruction. The agonized question of how to understand such horrors as the German concentration camps is answered by the poet's conviction that one must recognize the violence in oneself, bring it to light, and see it as having creative, not just destructive power. In "The Time of Burning" Kali is asked to "be with us":

> Help us to be the always hopeful
> Gardeners of the spirit
> Who know that without darkness
> Nothing comes to birth
> As without light
> Nothing flowers.

Parts II and III provide a kind of light interlude between the two more serious sections of the book. They contain poems on animals; on scenes in France and Holland; and reflections on music, friendship, and particular people. Part IV has poems on religion, more deeply searching than any of Miss Sarton's previous ones on the subject. In most of them the speaker has suffered some terrible agony of spirit, a personal hell; and the poems express a need to emerge from the numbing silence and enclosure of that suffering to regain balance and vision.

As in the earlier volume, *A Private Mythology,* the longing for faith, with its healing power, is expressed sometimes in images of birth or rebirth. In "The Silence," newly born lambs and the sheep's "throaty cry of hunger and arrival" say to the speaker that "raw grief" may be a prelude to some fulfillment. In "The Annunciation," the gravity of the angel speaks of pain; but beyond the pain is a resurrection:

> Joy is announced as if it were despair.
> Mary herself could do nothing to save,
> Nothing at all but to believe and bear,
> Nothing but to foresee that in the ending
> Would lie the true beginning and the birth,
> And all be broken down before the mending.

Two poems about Chartres show the poet's awareness of God's majesty and mercy and also his demand on the human spirit.

Two of the most effective poems in this section, "A Hard Death" and "Beyond the Question," use the image of a flower dropping its petals as a symbol of a way in which loss can be accepted and the grief of loss transcended. In "Beyond the Question," the poet sees a white peony become, as the magical soft petals fall, only a "stiff, five-pointed seed"; she wonders, could it not have been kept intact for another moment? The answer comes swiftly:

> Creation itself
> Tears the fabric apart,
> In the instant of achievement
> Makes new demands.

In "A Hard Death," she speaks of anemones and roses withering so imperceptibly that one can see no change, yet actually each flower is "flying through space, doing a dance / Toward the swift fall of petals, all at once."

Her conclusion, in both poems, is that destruction and death must be accepted—they are a part of the human condition—but that beyond what we can see and understand, we can know by intuition the infinite love and creative purpose of God. The answer to the question of violence and suffering is found in gentleness and faith—a conclusion set forth in the third stanza of "A Hard Death":

We cannot save, be saved, but we can stand
Before each presence with gentle heart and hand;
Here in this place, in this time without belief,
Keep the channels open to each other's grief;
Never accept a death or life as strange
To its essence, but at each second be aware
How God is moving always through each flower
From birth to death in a multiple gesture
Of abnegation; and when the petals fall
Say it is beautiful and good, say it is well.

VII *Desire for Perfection*

Considering all of Miss Sarton's poetry, from the publication of
Encounter in April in 1937 to *A Grain of Mustard Seed* thirty-
four years later, one sees how, in one form or another, the desire
for perfection runs through her poems. Perfection in both life and
art is the goal; for, indeed, she thinks of the two as inseparable.
In several essays and lectures about the writing of poetry, and in
her novel, *Mrs. Stevens Hears the Mermaids Singing* (1965),
she has made more explicit the idea that the poems imply—
that the journey toward perfection is made by the poet in both
his life and his works. She thinks of poetry, not as a profession
that can be kept separate from "personal" life, but as a way of
life itself. W. B. Yeats and Paul Valéry are, she says, the two
poets who have most influenced her, and both of them wished to
have no separation between poetry and life.[8]

As a young apprentice in the theater, Miss Sarton learned the
value of devotion to an art. Many years later, she said, speaking
to students at Scripps College, that the writing of poetry is "a life
discipline . . . maintained in order to perfect the instrument of
experiencing—the poet himself." [9] As the poet grows in experience, he ideally becomes more sensitive and aware, and his
poetry reflects changes in his inner state. But some themes, she
believes, he explores throughout his life. Always he serves poetry
"as a good servant serves his master"; he "must revere and woo
it as the mystic reveres and woos God through self-discipline
toward joy. . . ." [10]

A word that she uses a number of times in speaking of both
poetry and the poet's life is *tension.* Just as every great poem
contains "tension in equilibrium," the same "perilous equilib-

rium" exists, she believes, in the life of every poet. In a talk at
the Johns Hopkins Poetry Festival in 1961, she spoke of a permanent tension between being a public and a private person: to
what extent should a poet submit to increasing pressures to
lecture, review other people's books, and give time to being a
public figure? She believes that a poet is also aware of tension
between art and life and between the living and the dead.[11] And
always, in art, if not in life, the necessary balance is achieved
only temporarily—for the stress of working toward it is in itself
the stuff of poetry. Who would, to use her words, "bind the
dragon" permanently, when this dragon of intense feeling produces the poem? In a humorous treatment of this idea, she gives
a dialogue between the highly emotional poet and the "cautious
analyst" who advises him to sublimate his feelings. The last
stanza reads:

> He did not want the dragon to be caught.
> He wanted it alive and in his fist.
> For who would kill the god with whom he fought?
> And so he wept and cursed the analyst.[12]

And yet, the perilous balance must be constantly sought. In his
life and in his art, the poet aspires to a condition like that of the
saints, a detached joy. The state is treated in most detail in *In
Time Like Air*, but it is sometimes described in a few lines, as in
these near the end of her "Letter from Chicago for Virginia
Woolf." [13] Here the speaker wonders if his highest achievement
is this joy that comes paradoxically out of a sense of great loss:

> Is it to be poised as the lake beside the city,
> Aloof, but given still to air and wind,
> Detached from time, but given to the moment . . . ?

Perhaps Miss Sarton's best prose statement of the idea is in an
article published in 1966: "Poetry . . . demands a very delicate
and exhausting balance between . . . feeling and thought, between becoming and being, between the ultra-personal and the
universal—and these balances are shifting all the time." [14]

But, if art and life are, in a sense, inseparable, how does life
become art? Miss Sarton believes that the poet's intense self-
awareness, his sense of balancing his own "becoming and being,"
set him apart from other people. For, though she thinks of poetry

as a way of life, she sees the artist as different—detached from life and always a bit suspect, sometimes considered an actual enemy. Her character Mrs. Stevens says in *Mrs. Stevens Hears the Mermaids Singing* that "the creative person, the person who moves from an irrational source of power, has to face the fact that this power antagonizes. Under all the superficial praise of the 'creative' is the desire to kill" (169).

VIII   *Nature and Source of Poetic Inspiration*

Published in 1965, *Mrs. Stevens Hears the Mermaids Singing* is an unusual novel, different from all of Miss Sarton's others, for its chief concern is not relationships among human beings but ideas about the nature and sources of poetic inspiration. Mrs. Stevens is an elderly poet, and her hearing the mermaids is symbolic of the various times when the Muse imposed its demands on her—compelled her to write.

The story thread is slight, at least insofar as what outwardly "happens"; for the real "action" occurs as Mrs. Stevens remembers. Mrs. Stevens, who lives a retired life in a house at Cape Ann, Massachusetts, receives two interviewers from New York, who have come to question her about her work, now that, after years of only partial recognition, she has at last become famous. When she awakens on the day of the interview, she feels disturbed by the thought of the ordeal. Her concern is that she answer their questions honestly because in doing so she will be forced to confront herself—to face some of the disturbing things about herself and her past. Her reminiscences during the morning are of her marriage (ended many years ago with the premature death of Adrian) and of her childhood, her mother and father. As she prepares for the interview by searching the past, she also thinks of the present—of Mar, the young man who is troubled about a homosexual relationship which can be coped with, she tells him, by writing poetry. When he comes to work in her garden, they have long, passionate discussions about writing; and she finds her own poetry improving as the boy learns to write.

The second part of the book describes the interviewers, Peter Selversen and Jenny Hare, who, driving up to Cape Ann, wonder what Mrs. Stevens will be like. They are young, eager, and a bit nervous at the prospect of their assignment—to find out from her, if they can, the origin of her poetry; what has kept her at writing all these years? Jenny has written a novel herself and is worried by the current attitude toward women writers. Why is it not possible, she asks Peter and herself, to be a wife and mother and also an author? Must a woman who writes forgo a normal life?

The first section of the novel, then, introduces the reader to Hilary Stevens; the second, to the interviewers. The third and longest part is called "The Interview." In it, the questions that Peter and Jenny ask about her writing cause Hilary to continue the introspective searching begun in the morning, and the story moves between conversations of the three and flashbacks in Hilary's mind. The young reporters are, throughout, a bit in awe of Hilary; but they are courageous and ask questions that not only will give them an article about the springs of genius but also will enable Hilary to face some of her own conflicts and understand herself. After a preliminary chat over tea, the interviewers begin by asking how the momentum for writing comes—what causes one to write?

Hilary walks to the window where she stands, reflecting for about five minutes. She remembers a summer in Wales, when she was fifteen; here the Muse made her first appearance, for Hilary fell in love with her governess, Phillippa Munn; finding out painfully that Phillippa would never step out of her role as mentor to show any affection, the child finally discovered in writing poems an outlet for her pent-up emotion. The whole excruciating experience was then buried by her in her subconscious mind, but it reappeared in the form of her first novel written five years later, after her marriage to Adrian.

During her illness that followed Adrian's death, Hilary learned from a hospital doctor how to use personal emotion—not just to transpose it as she had done in her novel but to use the energy that it generates and write poetry that is apparently objective. In this experience, the Muse was Nurse Gillespie, "with her austere closed face and clear blue eyes" (119). Hilary's attachment to her was noticed by Dr. Hallowell, who with great understanding and appreciation of her sensitivity, urged her to write about objects instead of people. Nurse Gillespie, like all the other women who have been the Muse for Hilary, was someone who "captured the imagination" (121).

The next person she remembers, after the reporters ask

whether the Muse is always incarnate, an actual person, is Willa MacPherson. Partly through discovering a buried grief in Willa's life, Hilary was drawn into a new intimacy with her and began to write poems for her, which Willa in her turn discussed and criticized, so that the relationship was a "strange marriage of two minds" (146), which ended by Hilary's forcing her intense love on Willa in a way that brought on a stroke. The pain of recalling this far-off experience is so great that, when Hilary returns to the reporters, they notice her white face and fear they are tiring her.

But she valiantly continues the discussion about changes in her style in the various books of poems. Those with a markedly musical tone were inspired, she tells them, by the singer Madeleine HiRose. But the collection called *Dialogues*, which Peter says is a "queer cold book" (161), came from Hilary's involvement with Dorothea, another embodiment of the Muse. Here the love was always mixed with warfare, a struggle for Hilary's own identity and value; for Dorothea, as a sociologist, challenged the poet's "incredibly personal" (162) approach to life.

Toward the end of the interview, the reporters return to the question of whether a woman can be an artist and at the same time a successful wife and mother. Hilary Stevens believes that woman's natural creation is children; and, when she feels driven to create works of art, she does so "at the *expense* of herself as a woman" (191). But the important thing is that she be herself, "a whole person," whether or not she marries.

The last part of the book, the epilogue, concerns the boy Mar. Since Hilary's concern about him is revealed early in the novel, his personality and his problems give a framework to the whole book. When he comes to see her on the morning after the interview, he tells her that he has tried sex without love—he spent the night with a sailor in a shabby hotel—and he is bitterly unhappy. Hilary realizes with a shock that Mar has been to her an image of herself—the boy she wanted to be—but that her way of using chaotic passion should not be his. Although he can write poetry, she feels it is more important for him to marry instead of choosing, as she did, "the path of the impossible transcended" (218).

Certainly this novel lacks action in the usual sense of the word. When it appeared, some reviewers felt that it was not a novel at all but a discussion of creative writing; and others were embarrassed by the references to homosexuality. Mar's adventures, however, though similar in a sense to some of Hilary's, serve only to emphasize one theme of the book—the variety and complexity of love, its many forms and guises. And love for the artist can be the means of creation. Love and art have been the chief concerns of Hilary Stevens' life, and the action of the novel is her coming to realize their true relationship. Miss Sarton says of the novel that it is "a picaresque novel in which all the adventures are inward." [15] In such a sense the action is full of interest and suspense; various embodiments of the Muse appear only once, but the thread of Hilary's understanding of herself is strengthened with each recollection.

And, in the end, Hilary's character makes the book. The subjective quality of the action, the emphasis on idea above story— these set the novel apart from Miss Sarton's other fiction, where there is a complex interrelationship of characters and understanding of many personalities. In *Mrs. Stevens*, only Hilary really comes to life. Peter and Jenny, even Mar, who is treated at greater length, serve only to set her life and motives in sharper outline. She lives and breathes: the reader knows her "light laugh," her trick of ending sentences with "don't you know?" He sees her intensity of feeling and her passion for orderliness. He sees her, in the backflashes, as angry and tormented and in moods of both ecstasy and despair. And yet, like the interviewers, he finds her still a mystery—a person who is "advancing and retreating at the same instant, both transparent and secret . . ." (87).

The sense of her being different and the awe that the reporters feel in her presence are not just the result of Hilary's fame and achievement; they derive from Miss Sarton's belief that the artist stands apart from "ordinary" life. In Hilary Stevens she has created a character comparable to Tonio Kröger in Thomas Mann's story of that name: someone who cannot be a part of usual life because he is driven to create. Mrs. Stevens implies that her kind of creation involves as much pain and suffering as childbearing, but to produce the work of art she inevitably sacrifices some human qualities in her personal life. Art and life are related but immensely different. Speaking of her attachment to the Muse, Hilary says this kind of love is not that which makes a good marriage. The Muse is associated with "love as the waker of the dead, love as conflict, love as the mirage. Not love as peace or fulfillment, or lasting, faithful giving" (156). Art is seen, therefore, as a hard and demanding master, for it requires for itself all that is best in an unusually sensitive and loving individual.

If *Mrs. Stevens* lays chief stress on the difference of the artist from other people, it also makes clear how vastly different is the work of art from the life of which it is made. Hilary speaks of the two in one of her "lapidary" statements: " 'May we agree that private life is irrelevant? Multiple, mixed, ambiguous at best—out of it we try to fashion the crystal clear, the singular, the absolute, and that is what *is* relevant; that is what matters' " (125). This idea is familiar to readers of Miss Sarton's poetry, for she is constantly fascinated by the contrast between the transience and wild turbulence of life and by the permanence of the work of art—its stillness that contains the turbulence in memorable form. The best examples of this contrast are in *The Lion and the Rose* and in *The Land of Silence*. One recalls, for example, the end of "Boy by the Waterfall," where the momentary illusion of a perfect work of art vanishes when the boy does not dive a second time; "real life" has returned:

> Now there is only silence.
> There is no connection any more between the pool
> And the boy, between the actual image and the vision.
> Dream and reality are parted.
> > There is only,
> > without end, division.[16]

Why a poet writes has been explored by Miss Sarton. In *Mrs. Stevens*, it is chiefly pain and grief that urge the poem into being. Emphasis in the novel is placed on how the tensions of life are transposed into the energy of the poem, and Hilary Stevens puts less stress than her author does on the joy that belongs to writing. But, in a letter to a beginning poet, Miss Sarton says that poets are people "who work for joy alone"; they write because they have to and "even glory is a by-product." [17] Nor is the joy for the poet alone: by writing, he communicates a greater sense of life to other people; he makes them more fully human: "For poetry exists to break through to below the level of reason where the angels and monsters that the amenities keep in the cellar may come out to dance, to rove and roar, growling and singing, to bring life back to the enclosed room where too often we are only 'living and partly living.'" [18] The poet also writes, she says, to understand his own experience. Hilary Stevens tells the boy Mar that writing poetry means putting the chaos of feeling into order. "Making a poem," she says, "is . . . the ordering, the understanding of feeling" (31).

One of Miss Sarton's favorite words about the poet is "transparency," by which she means honesty with oneself and with others, a refusal to wear any mask of hypocrisy or conventionality, and therefore a willingness to be hurt or changed by experience. The poet must not try to protect himself but must suspend his will and be "an instrument . . . open to any accidental and fortuitous event." [19] The poet, far from being enclosed in an ivory tower, is keenly sensitive to life; he is "awake." In speaking to students, Miss Sarton often quotes Thoreau's comment, "To be awake is to be alive. I have never yet met a man who was quite awake. How could I have looked him in the face?" The state of being aware and transparent is one that must be cultivated, she believes; she herself finds that she needs often to rest instead of enjoying social pleasures, so that the fine edge of awareness may not become blunted.[20]

IX *Theory and Practice*

Turning from Miss Sarton's theory of poetry to her actual practice, one finds in her selected poems a great variety of both tone and form. Often the mood is thoughtful and questioning, as in "Somersault," which begins, "Not to rebel against what pulls us down / The private burdens each of us could name. . . ." The serious, half-wistful tone here is typical of many of the meditative poems, such as "Humpty-Dumpty," "The Work of Happiness," and "Letter to an Indian Friend." In contrast, there are basically serious poems that have a wry humor at the speaker's expense; such are "The Phoenix" and "The Frog, That Naked Creature." In the series of sonnets entitled "These Images Remain," there is a sense of serenity, of strong feeling severely controlled. The tone of "Summer Music" is airy and joyous; that of "Nativity" is a different joy, impersonal and full of awe. Some poems, like "The Tree," are written from a child's viewpoint and are wondering and delighted. In "Evening in France" a mood of dreamy peace is evoked by a series of pictures.

She shows a decided preference for strict metrical form, believing that creative energy is not held back by form but released by it. Formal structure has, for her, "satisfied the need for the absolute." [21] When a poem in regular form has finally been finished, she can say, "All is held solid and clear and contained; there is nothing ragged or spilled over. I can hold it in my hand like a rock." [22] This statement seems particularly significant in the light of her frequent use of images of formality in the poems —the "vision locked in stone"; the window that frames immensity; the light of every season flowing between trees statuesque as temple columns; the severe perspective in "Annunciation," where "This narrowing path is drawn to set us free, / Sends us to Heaven curiously designed"; and the feeling that pervades both "Italian Garden" and "The Metaphysical Garden"—of something vast and powerful contained in formal outlines. She has so often used images of architecture (columns, arches, open squares, enclosed spaces, walled paths) that it is as if, together, the architectural image and metrical form can best accomplish her ambition, "To hold eternally present and forever still / The always fugitive, to make the essence clear. . . ." [23]

After the sonnet, her favorite metrical form is the quatrain, but she sometimes uses stanzas of other lengths—five to nine lines. And, of course, in each poem the form is determined by the idea and by what Miss Sarton, quoting Jacques Maritain, calls "the musical stir" that "begins its rhythmic buzzing in the poet's mind" [24] and causes the first words to be written. A close examination of any of her poems shows how the idea has created the form. For example, the long, six-beat line in "Homage to Flanders" gives a feeling of stretches of low, flat land, where the sky with its marching clouds is the most noticeable feature of the landscape. Similarly, in "Charleston Plantations" the six-beat line makes the reader feel he is penetrating farther and farther into the desolate, swampy land where the empty houses are rotting away. As if under a spell, he goes

> Down the long avenues where mosses cover up the leaves,
> Across the empty terraced lawns neglected and asleep,
> To the still place where no dog barks and no dove grieves,
> And a black mirror gives you back your face too white . . .

In sharp contrast, a trimeter line is used to show the simplicity and striking contrasts in Provence:

> The shadows are all black,
> The sun intensely white,
> And between this and that
> No cloud or motion, but
> Irradiating light.

The use of dimeter in "On a Winter Night" suggests bareness and a kind of mysterious desolation; the poem begins:

> On a winter night
> I sat alone
> In a cold room,
> Feeling old, strange
> At the year's change
> In fire light.

And for a feeling of knitting together, erasing the sense of exile through an all-encompassing love, the sestina is the perfect form for "From All Our Journeys."

Miss Sarton believes that rhyme is the "least important element in English poetry," much less so than "the shape and weight of the poem as a whole." [25] Some of her poems give an impression of rhyming without actually doing so, and many depend on regular meter alone, using irregular rhymes. This stanza from "The Land of Silence" illustrates the latter type of poem:

> Now I am here in the land of silence,
> Of the near dove and the distant hills,
> I know that the surface is the essence,
> No stripping down what is already bare,
> No probing what is absolutely here.
> This is the land of bones and violent dreaming
> Where Heaven is woven in and out of Hell
> And each not essence but actual and near.

In almost all of the poems, her preference is for near rhymes (such as *bare* rhyming with *here* in the preceding selection) or for a rhyming effect produced by consonance or assonance. In "The Action of the Beautiful," for example, *presence* is rhymed with *balance* and *radiance*; and in this first stanza of "These Were Her Nightly Journeys" various *o* sounds in the end words produce a delicate music that is more effective than rhyme:

These were her nightly journeys made alone,
The prisoners of seas which cannot drown,
Forced to descend the vertical
Plunges of dream.
Though all day long she knew no fear would come
And freely walked (who once in dreams had flown)
At night, she fell.
Burdens returned to magnetize the bone,
And in her helpless sleep she was hurled down.

The two short lines in this stanza emphasize the violence of the dream experience. A few poems, such as "In Time Like Air" and "Nativity," have very intricate rhyme schemes, ones so subtle and unobtrusive as to seem almost like no rhyme at all. The rather long poem "The Lady and the Unicorn," suggested by the Cluny tapestries, uses in all the lines end words containing either the long or the short *e* sound; yet, without a close examination of its technique, the reader is aware only of a pleasant interweaving effect in keeping with the idea of a tapestry.

All of these examples illustrate what Miss Sarton means when she says, "I have wished always a deceptive clarity rather than a deceptive obscurity." [26] She has said also that "Poetry finds its perilous equilibrium somewhere between music and speech, and each poet as he comes along has to breathe his own breath, find his own intervals that will make it 'sound right' for him." [27] Her own voice is both gentle and powerful. It is a combination of keen perception and ordinary language used freshly, as in "the slow rising of the full moon / That delicate disturber of the soul." [28] It is metrical regularity and the "all-but-inaudible rhymes" [29] that together produce the subtle music and meditative mood characteristic of her best poetry. One may take Sonnets 17 and 18 of "Divorce of Lovers," a new series in *Cloud, Stone, Sun, Vine,* as in some ways typical of many previous poems. The first begins:

After a night of driving rain, the skies
Take on bright motion, radiant-obscure;
As thoughts like clouds traverse my human eyes,
Silence opens the world that I explore. . . .

Here the quiet tone, the exactness of observation remind one of the best of Wordsworth. A sense of reality that includes both the

objective world of things and events, and the subjective one of
the poet's mind is in this sonnet and is even more noticeable in
the next, for example in these lines:

> I feel
> The slightest change of air as an event,
> Attend to every creak of the old floor
> As to momentous words by angels sent,
> Inner and outer worlds, mine to explore.

Although these two selections are not entirely typical of this sonnet sequence (in which the grief of parting is more fiercely stated
that in any of the previous love poems), they are characteristic
of the great body of Miss Sarton's work. The word *explore* in
both of them indicates the careful analysis of experience in her
poetry; and the emphasis, in both, on the silent inner world is
typical of the thoughtfulness that often borders on the mystical
state.

To summarize Miss Sarton's ideas about poetry: she thinks of
it as a way of life, enormously demanding and to some extent
setting the poet apart from ordinary life; yet his detachment is
self-imposed, for he cherishes his differences, his sensitive awareness of life, and he realizes that along with his intensity he must
be coolly critical if he is to perfect his craft. Mrs. Stevens knows
that it will always be said of her, "you feel too much and you are
at the same time too detached to be quite human" (108). The
poet sacrifices some precious aspects of personal life, but his
transparency and his critical detachment from his own work
make it possible for him to widen his sympathies and grow in
skill as he grows in maturity as a person. The "sensation of things
opening out" is the tone of both *A Private Mythology* and *Plant
Dreaming Deep*.

Her achievement as a poet is impressive, and even more so is
her idealism about her art. In this respect, she is in the tradition
of Sir Philip Sidney and Percy Bysshe Shelley; but perhaps her
attitude toward poetry is best described in John Milton's words
about a book: "A good book is the precious life-blood of a master
spirit, embalmed and treasured up on purpose to a life beyond
life."

CHAPTER 3

The Early Novels: Detachment

BEFORE 1970, when *Kinds of Love* appeared, May Sarton's novels, other than *Mrs. Stevens,* may be divided into two groups, those in each group linked by both chronology and theme. The first four, published between 1938 and 1952, are all set wholly or partly in Europe; in two of them, the impact of Europe on America is vital to the plot. This concern with two worlds is natural in the poet who had written of the deep-rooted love of one's birthplace and of the pain of separation and exile. A common theme in these early novels is that of detachment, an idea prominent also in Miss Sarton's early poetry. In the second group of novels, written between 1955 and 1969, the setting of all except *Joanna and Ulysses* is New England; and in this group the need, not for detachment, but for communion is emphasized. Taken as a whole, the novels say that both detachment and communion are necessary for the good life; or, as the author suggested in several poems of *The Lion and the Rose,* "passion," after it has been detached from self-interest, may become "compassion." The lion of passion or youthful intensity is transmuted by detachment into both the rose of the poem and the rose of a spiritual love that can encompass all mankind.

I *The Single Hound* (1938)

Miss Sarton's first novel, *The Single Hound,* deals with poetry and love—subjects natural to the young writer who had just published her first book of poems. There is a hero, Mark Taylor, a young man who must learn to come to terms with his own passionate nature; and there is a heroine, the old Belgian poet named Doro, who helps Mark understand himself and the world. The title, taken from lines of Emily Dickinson, refers to the soul's being constantly attended by "a single hound— / Its own identity."

The story begins in Belgium, in a school run by three elderly women; and the reader of *I Knew a Phoenix* recognizes that this school is modeled, at least to some extent, on the one founded by Marie Closset, which Miss Sarton attended when she was twelve years old. Doro, frail and sensitive, with great expressive eyes, is physically like Marie Closset, and she teaches in somewhat the same manner: "She did not explain. She created an atmosphere by her very presence, and then gave them one by one the words she had brought with her. . . . She said, "Don't try to remember what I am reading. Try to feel it" (25). Doro's classes are extraordinary in their "capacity for exciting wonder."

Doro's companions are Claire—a widow whom she has known since they were schoolgirls, when Claire wrote fiction and they were, for a few months, inseparable—and Anne, who came into their lives later and who now does most of the practical work at the school and also most of the teaching. The three of them, called "The Little Owls," find their companionship, a joining of three separate solitudes, a delight. They laugh a great deal and enjoy simple pleasures—their tiny flower garden, their cat Pascal, their endless cups of tea, and the special treats on gala days.

Slight as these happenings are, the reader learns much about the three women, especially about Doro—her trouble with her eyes and her dizzy spells; her never-expressed love for a married man named Bird; her shyness that led her to publish her poems under the assumed name of Jean Latour; and her feeling that Watteau's white Clown, Gilles, is her Muse, the inspiration for all her poetry. The first part of the novel ends with each of the Little Owls going to bed; and Doro, who always has a moment of luminous vision just before sleep, feels on this night that something momentous is about to happen to her.

The second part, "Innocent Landscape," is concerned with the young poet, Mark Taylor. For some months he has been living alone in a friend's house in Rye in England. He is lonely and perplexed because his best friend, Al, who has joined the Communist party, has gone to fight in Spain. One evening he finds in the house a small book of poems by "Jean Latour" and is so moved by their truth for him that he resolves to go to Belgium to talk with the author, who must, he realizes, be an old man by now. He takes a train to London, where he spends the night with his editor-friend Carter. His journey to Belgium is delayed by a few days while he writes an article to earn money for his ticket. While in a restaurant with Carter, he meets Georgia Manning, the artist, and her husband; and he suddenly, romantically, and devastatingly falls in love with Georgia.

Now begins his anguished joy. Having, in great excitement, telephoned her, he goes to have tea with her and sees her landscape painting that he previously admired in an exhibit. She is disturbed by his intensity and by his unspoken thoughts; but, as she thinks of his trip to Belgium, she is certain that she will never see him again. Mark, however, has unintentionally left his hat behind; when he returns to get it, he tells her of his love and begs her to come to him at Carter's flat the next day. In the fullness of his passion, he longs, when she comes, to possess her soul as well as her body; and he finds the sweetness of their lovemaking terrible as well as good, for she must leave him again, and he realizes that he will never know a peaceful love with her. Georgia is shaken by the experience, remorseful at having caused his suffering; she promises to write to him; and she returns thankfully to her safe, orderly life with Manuele.

Mark, on his way at last to Belgium, realizes that he was wrong in his passionate longing to burst into Georgia's inner life. He reflects that "Without preparation, without reason, as one might take a bird in the hand, he had wanted to seize Georgia, possess her completely in one way or another—and every way had failed, the simple way of the hand and mouth, the subtle way of the imagination." This realization is accompanied by the conviction that he is "in some way wrong" in everything he has done, except in going to Belgium to find Jean Latour (154). It is as if Mark symbolizes man groping his way from sensuality and selfishness to a spiritual quality that he knows to be his also but cannot yet find. In bringing together Mark and Doro, the novelist is showing the two halves of man's nature.

Part III, "The Single Hound," describes Mark's arrival in Ghent and his meeting with Doro. She has answered his letter to Jean Latour without revealing her sex; but, as soon as he walks into the room where she is, Mark recognizes her as the poet, who could only have been a woman. She, in turn, is startled to realize that Mark looks exactly like her "Muse," the Watteau Gilles. From the first moment, there is perfect communication between them—sometimes by words, sometimes by silence. Mark feels that he has at last found himself; but he does not, on this first day, tell her about Georgia.

He has written to Georgia, who finds his letter sadly disturbing and sends an answer intended to comfort him; but it infuriates him in its lack of a love like his own. In angry impatience, he telephones and insists that she come to Ghent for one day. To quiet him, she promises to come; and, after telling Manuele that she must go there to paint a portrait, she justifies her deception by remembering that her real love is for Manuele and that the momentary intoxication of the affair with Mark must end—she hopes it can end without pain to him.

When Mark again visits the Little Owls, he realizes he has a new joy in his relationship to Doro; for it is in essence spiritual, "having to do, he saw now, with a way of life as well as a personality"; and this new kind of life "might be the answer to all personal despair: it might achieve for him what the embracing of communism had done for Al" (182). When he sees Doro this time, he tells her about his love for Georgia. Doro is not surprised; she understands suffering and makes him see that "everything that would happen to him now and for years to come would be like this, difficult and painful and in the end necessary" (212). He learns, from talking with her, that he must not, through the violence of passion, makes others suffer; he must learn to renounce. But he senses that the necessary detachment cannot be immediately attained. In Doro's room, or in her sheltered garden, everything became simple and possible; but "he knew that only for a moment would he be able to enter this garden, . . . only at moments would it seem good to love Georgia and ask for nothing . . ." (213).

He has to learn renunciation all over again when Georgia comes the next day, determined to tell him what her letter had been unable to convey—that she loves him but not as a lover does; that their lives from now on must be apart. And Mark, perhaps because Doro has opened a door for him into the spiritual world, understands at last that there can be love without possession—in fact, that love which has renounced passion is more complete and joyous than the tense pain-in-joy of passion.

When he goes again to see Doro, she tells him the weakness of his poem, which he has left for her to read. He is trying, in it, to be like other people; he has, he admits, been ashamed of "living in this personal world, because it seemed to me that I must lose myself in something greater" (235). She lets him know that, just as he must accept anguish, he must also accept himself and never pretend to be other than he is: for "death is the inevitable result for anyone who gives up his differences" (238). These are almost the last words she speaks to him. She feels that death is very near, and Mark receives a note that evening at his hotel from Claire informing him that Doro is ill and cannot see him again. Mark realizes how much she has given him, and he knows that now his own career is beginning.

The Single Hound was well received, not only as a promising novel from a young person, but in itself as an interesting treatment of some important ideas, particularly those about poetry. The poet's right to be "personal" was one idea singled out for comment by two reviewers. Equally interesting, in the light of *Mrs. Stevens,* is Doro's insistence that a poet (or, she implies, anyone) must be himself and not "give up his differences." Doro, Miss Sarton's first fictional treatment of the artist as vulnerable and "transparent," feels at age sixty-three "still so vulnerable, so expectant, so lonely, like a child wondering if she can get back home in the dark before the wolf will devour her" (67). Hers is the state of openness that Miss Sarton thinks essential if the poet is to produce good work. Mark, also, knows that he is different from other people, and he seeks out Doro as a kindred spirit. In his three months in the house in Rye "he had had a curious feeling of growing transparency. He almost wondered if he would ever veer back again to the opacity, the necessary walls of social personality" (77).

The pain of such transparency is felt by both the young poet and the old. They will never be "adjusted" to the world, for such adjustment would be the end of their poetry. Nor will Georgia, the painter, ever lose her tender heart, her intuitive understanding of the anguish of someone like Mark; for she, too, is different from most people. Looking at her landscape painting, Mark realizes that Georgia always feels a need to keep some part of herself hidden, and he wonders, "Was it that that gave her painting an impression of both hiding and revealing something? . . . She must, sometimes, have drawn back, have wanted to tear up a canvas once it was finished. And this curious tension between the tyranny of the art and her temperament gave excitement and point to everything she did" (153). She is, in fact, rather like Hilary Stevens, who gives the reporters the impression of simultaneously advancing and retreating. In her first novel as in *Mrs. Stevens*, Miss Sarton has seen the artist as someone with no "walls" who must either live in seclusion, as Doro does, or erect some kind of psychic defense that will enable him to channel the best of his emotional power into art rather than into life.

What the artist produces is "the elements of passion, but arranged for contemplation instead of action" (151). Such is Mark's thought as he looks at Georgia's landscape, and its is reminiscent of Miss Sarton's "vision locked in stone" and the other poems which speak of the diffuse passion of life that has been caught and held in art. In creating this memorable form, the artist gives up his own personal peace; he works with passion because only so can he work at all. Always, Mark thinks, "it is some dream of a quiet country that leads one to these passionate journeys—to be eternally deceived. Because the peace is the antithesis of the journey" (151).

Such ideas about the nature of poetry and the poet give the novel its chief value. As characters, the Little Owls are not quite real; though they are presented with great sympathy and beauty, they have no shadows, no weaknesses except amiable ones. Doro especially is highly idealized: she is like an allegorical figure representing man's spirit, and as such she is appealing. Her feeling of being encumbered by her body and her final realization that she does not fear death seem right and beautiful; but she does not quite come alive as a person. Mark, on the other hand, is what a reviewer called "a sturdy sensualist." [2] But he is not just allegorical; he is a more fully realized character than Doro, for he feels the attraction of the spiritual and moves toward it. His intensity of self-abnegation is poignant. Georgia also is completely believable, with her reserve, her hesitancy, her moods of exasperation with Mark and with the inevitable confusions and torments of life.

The relationship between Mark and Georgia emphasizes another idea frequently found in Miss Sarton's poetry—that passion and love are different; they exclude each other. Passion is seen as a violent, energizing force; it may be considered a joy but not happiness, which is a quieter and steadier thing. When Mark leaves Georgia for the second time, she tells him to be happy (she is already trying to shield him from the pain that will come); but Mark, knowing only that he will see her again the next day, thinks, "Happiness is her word, not mine. Happiness is hers. I don't want it. Or at least my happiness is not this. It is lying on my stomach in the grass on a hot day. It is not this flood in the heart" (134).

Both of them, however, feel the surge of energy that comes from their momentary passion. Georgia knows, on the day when she is to go to Carter's flat to meet Mark, that her hands will be powerful as she paints that morning; it is as if a lamp had been lighted within her, and she can see more clearly. In the same way, Mark, in his little garret room in Ghent, finds that passion has given him new power to write. They both know that their relationship will be brief, but they are inspired by passion: "For the moment Georgia had found the peak. For the moment Mark across the channel had found it. Temporary security of this kind is precious. Each silently and alone used it, set it down in paint, in words" (174). But such passion is not like the more peaceful love that even Mark experiences after Georgia has come to Ghent and refused to have him as her lover any more. Now they feel, having given up the "peak," that they can be easy and natural; that they can laugh together; and that each can learn something of the other's inner life. Just as passion is not happiness, neither is it love, the luminous thing that in an early poem Miss Sarton had described as "lying between us like a little child."

The style of *The Single Hound* is, on the whole, too self-consciously "poetic." Though there are passages showing excellent observation, the treatment of the characters' thoughts shows the awkwardness of a young novelist feeling her way into her craft. This awkwardness is not so much apparent in the parts dealing with the household in Ghent, but it mars those concerning Mark and Georgia, as in this passage immediately preceding Mark's declaration of love:

"You have come back for your h-h-hat." (Now the unreal becomes real. This is the dream. He is standing in the door. He is here.)
"Yes, you're working. I won't stay." (She is blushing. The real

becomes unreal. The careful preparation crumbles. She is blushing. I am dreaming now.) (127)

Not only the too-obvious play upon the words "real" and "unreal"
but also the placement of the thoughts of each person in parentheses makes the reader aware of technique. The parentheses and
the present tense together destroy the illusion; it is as if, when
one watched a puppet show, the hand of the puppeteer inadver-
tently appeared on the stage.

II *The Bridge of Years* (1946)

In her second novel, *The Bridge of Years,* published eight years
after *The Single Hound,* Miss Sarton used a much more complex
theme and treated it in more depth. This novel, set entirely in
Belgium, deals with the impact of two world wars on the Duchesne family. The story actually covers the period between the
wars, as Part I takes place in 1919, and the last part ends in the
spring of 1940, when the Germans are bombing Brussels.
Throughout the first war, Paul and Melanie Duchesne remained
on their small "family estate" near Brussels; though larger, the
house with its garden is rather like that of the Little Owls, with
a white table and chairs out under the apple tree and everywhere
a feeling of serenity, order, and beauty.

Paul works at home, as he is a philosopher and writer; he
hopes, now that the war is over, he may at last get his book published. Melanie goes daily to Brussels, where she manages the
family business, Maison Bernard, that deals in house furnishings.
The world of 1919 is gloomy. Instead of joy and prosperity that
had been hoped for with the end of war, there are poverty, un-
rest, and new problems. Melanie has few customers; she and her
assistants struggle with accounts and try to keep the business
solvent. But in the evening when she returns home she casts off
her worries and rejoices in seeing Paul and their five-year-old
daughter, Françoise. Bo-Bo, the head servant, is also like part of
the family, as are Lou-Lou and Marie, her helpers, and old Croll,
the gardener.

Through Croll's son, Jacques, the Duchesnes are made acutely
aware of the psychological havoc of the war. Jacques has returned from the army with what is called "war sickness," a terrible lethargy and despondency. Melanie, always eager to help

people in need, persuades Jacques to come and work in their garden. He comes; and, though he sleeps and idles more than he works, he at least is not so hopeless as before. But one day when Françoise, who has become attached to him, takes him into the house, he steals a jade rabbit, leaving Françoise in a dilemma that makes her almost ill: she dares not tell all she knows for fear of getting Jacques into trouble. At last she confesses to her father, who is furious to think that his child has been made to suffer. But Melanie will not turn Jacques over to the police; she feels that, if he is treated as a criminal, he will become one. Instead, she takes him to work at Maison Bernard to show that she still has faith in him. He gradually comes to feel safe with her, and her care and patience save him from a life of futility.

For Melanie and Paul, Jacques comes to symbolize all the returned soldiers who feel bewildered, despairing, unwanted by the country they had fought for. Paul reflects that "The truly heroic struggles come after the war is over," for then "the full ugliness of war, the waste, the destruction is visible in the living rather than the dead, terrible as their numbers may be" (57–58). Even the child Françoise is affected by the tension. In her "house" under the rhododendron bush, she wonders, "What was 'the war'? . . . why, if the good people had won, / did they seem so sad when they talked about it and often get angry . . ." (69).

The effect of war is seen dramatically again in the visit to Paul of his German friend Gerhart Schmidt. Paul thinks at first that nothing has changed between them, that Gerhart is exactly the same, as in many ways he is—still deeply interested in Paul's writing, he gives his usual sympathetic attention to the intricacies of Paul's thought. Yet sometimes silence falls between them, and both Paul and Melanie realize that they do not know Schmidt's real feelings about the war. Even worse, Marie and Lou-Lou refuse to serve a meal to Schmidt. Melanie sends them upstairs like naughty children; but they are unrepentant, for his coming brings back to them the grief of the war and the loss of their relatives. They cannot think of any German as quite human.

Here Miss Sarton makes one of the points emphasized in her poem "To the Living"—the idea that imagination is needed to heal old wounds, such as those left by war. For simple people like Lou-Lou and Marie, "Germany was a great evil mystery too far off to be recognized as human. They did not see the starving children in the streets of Berlin." What cannot be seen in actuality, the author suggests, must be seen by an effort of the imagination; for "the fact is that suffering does not make for generosity. Only imagination makes for generosity, only the acceptance that revenge was never the answer to human suffering—but only sandpaper on an abrasion, keeping the wound raw" (75–76). Gerhart Schmidt tells the Duchesnes of the incredible misery and hopelessness of the Germans, and Paul and Melanie understand; but they represent a small minority. The great masses, people like Lou-Lou and Marie, keep resentment alive through the stories of deaths in war. Even time, Paul and Melanie reflect, will be slow in healing the wound, for "how many bloody stories told at the hearths of farms in the long winter evenings would keep them alive; how often would the blood drip on the stone and imaginations burn with hate!" (75).

The theme of old wounds kept open is one of the most important in the novel; the remembrance of suffering and death, carried from one generation to another, is, in fact, one of the "bridges" linking past to present. Paul, who is rather a cynic, believes that an organization like the League of Nations cannot succeed just after a war because people are incapable so soon of forgetting. "You would," he says, "have to eliminate the fallibility of human nature first—to eliminate revenge, to start *tabula rasa,* as if there had been no war. But that is just what none of us is capable of doing. We are inextricably involved in the past" (44).

Yet remembrance of the past is also a helpful "bridge." The intellectual companionship of Paul and Gerhart Schmidt, established before the war, has not been destroyed. After Schmidt returns to Germany, Paul is stimulated to take up his writing again and finish his book; it has taken on a focus through his need to communicate his ideas fully to his friend. He begins to write with a concentration that shuts out the family completely, and for three weeks Melanie feels that he is unaware of their presence. When he finally finishes the book, she and Françoise rejoice in his "return." The first part of the novel ends with the gay reunion.

Five other characters have appeared in the first part: Francis and Simone La Grange come now and then to visit the Duchesnes; Simone and Melanie are old friends, deeply attached to each other; and Francis and Paul argue often about politics.

Francis, a confirmed optimist, is sure that the League of Nations will work and that war will henceforth be impossible. His discussions with Paul to keep the reader aware of the undercurrent of tension in the world which is sometimes lost sight of in the happiness of the Duchesne household. The couple Emile and Suzanne Poiret have a child Pierre, who is Françoise's age; but he is being reared in a quite different manner. Where Françoise is spanked for misbehavior, Pierre is gently "reasoned with" by his father, who cannot bear any kind of violence. Because Françoise is lonely, the Duchesnes suggest that Suzanne and Emile send little Pierre to them for long summer visits; and he becomes almost like another member of the family.

Part II of the novel takes place in the summer of 1930. Françoise is now "a gangling fifteen-year-old, reading Tolstoy" (92). And there are two other girls—Colette, conceived on the night that Paul's book was finished, and Solange, who came two years later. They are referred to as "the little ones." Paul, whose book was published but received no notice at all, has gone to work helping Melanie at the Maison Bernard. Pierre, who is making another summer visit and who is reading Lenin, is fond of Françoise, who ignores him. She loves Jacques, who thinks of her as only a child. Jacques courts Lou-Lou in a haphazard manner, for he does not want to settle down. He still works at Maison Bernard and has become very handsome.

Françoise's feelings, the difficulties and agonies of her adolescence, form one chief theme of this part. She resents her father and mother, who seem always to be asking too much of her: they "expected her to be good and generous and gentle when it was all she could do to keep from hitting everyone, hitting the world. . . . How did people go on living when it was so hard?" (96). She feels that her father, especially, sees too much of her anguish; and, although she loves him, she wants to shut him out; she longs for privacy and freedom. Above all, she longs for Jacques's love; but he, unconscious of her feeling for him, once calls her "Franci, darling" but immediately afterward blasts her hopes by saying, "You might tell Lou-Lou that I'll be round tomorrow night." This incident climaxes her misery, for "in a few seconds all was illuminated and then all blasted. In the darkness the child towered into a woman" (130). From then on, she withdraws more and more into her private world.

The remembrance of war is stressed again when Gerhart's son, Hans, visits the Duchesnes during this summer. The little ones dislike him before the comes—he is a German, "the enemy" they have heard of who invaded Belgium in 1914. Pierre, who has been reading and thinking, tells them that all the atrocity stories were Allied propaganda; there is nothing wrong with being a German. When Hans arrives, he is so attractive—"brown and fair and shy" (114)—that they all love him; and, for a few weeks, they live happily like one big family. But, near the end of the summer as tension mounts, Lou-Lou, in a temper, calls him "You little German!" (119); Hans, profoundly shocked, thinks that all the kindness of the Duchesnes has really been a sham.

The difference between him and the others is increased when they listen to one of Hitler's ranting speeches on the radio. Paul, Melanie, and Pierre think it fanatical and foolish, but Hans is deeply moved, even though he sees that Hitler's appeal is purely emotional. He feels, that night, "that his bed was a ship and he was sailing away very fast, sailing away from everything here, but he wanted to stay. . . . He didn't want to be carried off" (124). Eventually, what had begun as a happy friendship, with only goodwill on both sides, explodes into anger and misery. Pierre and Hans fight in a wood where they have gone with the "little ones" for a picnic. None of them reveal to the adults what has happened, and Hans and Pierre leave for home.

Another tension in the family is created by Paul's sense of failure. Though working at Maison Bernard, he still longs to write and be published. He confides his sadness, not to Melanie, but to Mlle Louvois, one of the assistants in the business. His desire to protect his wife from pain leads him to spend hours talking to the older woman about himself as well as about her unhappy love affair. But Melanie feels the lack of communication between herself and Paul. Even in the midst of troubles, however, she and Paul know that theirs is a good marriage and a good life. Part II ends with the wedding of Jacques and Lou-Lou.

In Part III, set in autumn, 1936, the war draws closer. Paul receives a letter from Gerhart Schmidt, saying that he wishes to leave Germany because of Nazi restrictions on his teaching. He asks if the University of Brussels can invite him to lecture. Hans, he says, has become a Nazi; and his wife will not leave their son, so Gerhart must leave both family and country. Paul arranges for an invitation to be sent from the university, and then they can only wait for news of Schmidt's arrival. Melanie feels that she must work harder to prepare her children for the future: "They must grow up strong and free and powerful in love—for what a weariness of hatred lay ahead she was beginning to understand, though she did not yet name it 'war'" (194–95).

At the business, Paul's relationship to Mlle Louvois comes to a climax. He has known of her adoration and felt guilty; for him, she is only someone to whom he can talk about his sense of failure. They have become a habit for each other, and Mlle Louvois also feels guilty because she too is loyal to Melanie. One morning Paul tells her that he loves her. To his amazement, she answers that this is nonsense—she has only been useful; for suddenly she sees his friendship and sympathy for what they were. She is happy for the first time in years.

Pierre, meanwhile, is having trouble. He has left home and has become an ardent Communist. He hardly ever visits his parents, but they find out that he is deeply in debt and has been locked out of his hotel for not paying his bill. Emile comes to the Duchesnes for help, and Pierre finds his father there. Emile realizes that Pierre does not love him or Suzanne and that it is their own fault, for they have brought him up badly, trying to "be his conscience" and not allowing him to be himself. Pierre, who did indeed feel his home to be a prison, weeps on finding that his father at last understands.

Paul and Melanie, waiting for word from Schmidt, feel like Noah before the flood. Yet the continuing sense of crisis helps to clarify their own relationship, perhaps because they feel there is to be little or no future. When Schmidt finally escapes from Germany and arrives at the Brussels airport, the whole family is wild with joy; but, after hearing his story, they know that war is now very close. Schmidt explains how the ordinary citizen has gradually come to accept the Nazi regime. The stories of suffering Jews are not heard in Germany except now and then, and an isolated case can be explained away as perhaps due to police brutality. "'And each time one has made the excuse, silenced one's conscience, it is a little easier the next time. So that now, after three years, things that no one could have accepted in the beginning seem almost inevitable'" (258). Listening to Schmidt, Collette decides that she must become a doctor; and Pierre feels that all his life so far has been wasted.

As the weeks go by, Schmidt feels more and more keenly that, having left his country, he must not just live in comfort but do what he can to help the struggle for freedom. Against Paul's protests, he leaves for Spain to fight the Fascists there.

In Part IV, in the winter of 1940, war has been declared. Belgium and Holland, the neutral countries, are heavily armed, waiting in terrible suspense. Gerhart Schmidt, the Duchesnes had learned, was killed in 1938 in Madrid. In 1939, Paul began to write, putting his reflections into a long letter to Schmidt, "a cry of despair and recognition across the silence" (279). Pierre is an officer in the Belgian army; Colette is at the university. Solange, having finished her course at the agricultural college, can now help to support the family. Françoise is a designer at Maison Bernard. Melanie feels that the children, for all their affection, have now withdrawn into their own lives.

The impact of Nazism comes through Ado, a friend of Colette's at the university. Ado begins a Fascist anti-Semitic group. When Colette protests at a meeting the attacks on Jews, she is ostracized by Ado and his friends. Colette, who loves Ado, is torn now between loyalty to him and hatred of his new ideas. Melanie protests to the rector of the university, to Ado's mother, and to Francis, but nobody can or will help. Colette, remembering what Schmidt had said about how easy it is to silence one's conscience, and determining not to do so, breaks off her friendship with Ado.

Paul reads his completed manuscript before fifty "friends of literature and philosophy" and to his amazement finds that he has communicated for the first time. There is great applause, and they crowd round him with questions and praises. He realizes that he has for the first time written with love; therefore, he has called forth love from others. He knows that he has Gerhart to thank for his ability to communicate; knowing what Gerhart sacrificed for his ideals of tolerance and mercy has broken the ice of cynicism within Paul.

One of the last incidents of the novel is the death of Moise, the goat, after a life of twenty years. Melanie feels it marks the end of an era of peace. On May 10, they hear the bombing over Brussels; all the reserves are called up; and people flee from Belgium. But the old and the sick cannot leave; people in the village need help;

and the Duchesnes refuse to go. Though they may be killed, they will not change their way of life.

As is apparent from the foregoing summary, war provides the chief unifying thread in *The Bridge of Years*. The arrangement of the four parts from spring to winter symbolizes the movement from lightness and hope after World War I to growing darkness and gloom as World War II approaches; and throughout the novel, it is either remembrance or anticipation of war that casts a shadow over the characters' lives. Though the reader's sympathy is enlisted chiefly for Belgium, it is the human rather than the political aspects of war that are emphasized; and in the character of Gerhart Schmidt—gentle, scholarly, perceptive—Miss Sarton has pictured the Germany that was never Hitler's. In warmth of heart and in nobility of ideals, Gerhart is equal to any of the Belgian characters. His son Hans, also attractive, is shown as too young and impressionable to resist the powerful persuasion of the Nazi doctrine.

With so much emphasis upon the tension and the suffering produced by war, the novel is remarkable for the absence of pessimism. The emphasis is not upon man as a victim of overwhelming forces of hate and destruction but upon man's ability to endure and, by sheer energy and joyousness, to overcome doubt and fear. How much he might do so in isolation is not broached by the author; rather, her intent is to show how a family, united by strong affection and by a common heritage, can be invincible. Each member of the Duchesne family finds in the "magical circle" of home a constant source of renewal: "Going out from it, they moved through the world armed in strength, warmed deep inside, with much to give because they burned brightly in themselves" (319).

The strength of the family is derived from one person—Melanie, the heart of the family and of the book. The others look to her for guidance and encouragement; and, without her, there would be "panic and emptiness and darkness instead of life and warmth and safety" (189). On the one occasion when she is ill for a week, Solange thinks of "how much Melanie held the whole fabric of their lives together. Without her, the garden, the house, the animals, the meals—everything seemed to have lost its reason for being" (189).

The secret of Melanie's charm is her gift of love. She responds to every need she is aware of. At the Maison Bernard, she inspires the workers not to lose hope, even when she herself can see no way of keeping the business solvent. She comforts Mlle Louvois, not as Paul does by philosophical truths, but by sitting on the arm of her chair and putting an arm around her, saying, "Allons, Mademoiselle, un peu de courage!" (114). Through Melanie's love and trust Jacques is able to throw off his "war sickness" and return to normal life. And Pierre Poiret as a fifteen-year-old "wished passionately that she were his mother, that he could run down the stairs and bury his head in her breast and tell her how much he loved her . . . how he would do something great in the world for her sake" (99–100). Later, when Pierre as a brash young Communist is shut out of his hotel, he walks in the park, half hoping Melanie will come to scold and rescue him, half dreading to see her because he has made a mess of his life.

The great reality of Melanie's character, developed by many small details, shows one how far Miss Sarton had developed as a writer in the eight years since her first novel. In *The Bridge of Years,* technique is unobtrusive; and every scene in which Melanie appears reveals her more fully. For example, one evening when she is upset and angry with herself, she comes into the kitchen, kisses the two girls, and wanders about "as if she had been away a long time and wanted to look at everything at once." Then,

> "That old pot needs scouring," she said, and characteristically, her hat and coat still on, her cooky unfinished, went to work on it. . . . Solange came behind her and took off her hat, teasingly, tenderly, and pulled at her coat till she could slip it off in spite of protests. Finally, as if Melanie had worked off some impatience, some despair, she turned to them triumphantly, showing the saucepan's shining bottom.
> "There, that's better." (316)

The style here is realistic and more effective than the rather self-consciously poetic style of *The Single Hound.*

Second only to Melanie in being fully realized, Paul Duchesne is another vivid character. He is quite different from his wife; where she may be said to represent the active life, he stands for the contemplative. His approach to life is the philosopher's: "this other kind of action, slow, and done in darkness like a miner digging coal, the effort to see clearly, to go deeply into every conflict that one might reach the universal answer . . ." (292). Yet even when most absorbed in his writing, he constantly wonders if he is right to be so "inactive." He is torn between what he calls "the life of the spirit" and "the spirit of life" (80); and his conflict is rather like that of Mrs. Stevens, who feels that the artist can never live as fully as other people do. Moreover, her life is devoted to poetry just as Paul's is devoted to philosophy. An interesting, and to Paul a rather appalling, result of his conflict is Colette's being unable to decide between becoming a doctor or a poet. When she asks her father how she can decide "between serving poetry and serving life itself" (203), he realizes that, with her unusual sensitivity, Colette has been "trying desperately to be both her mother and her father in one person" (205).

Paul's conflict is not only between the two approaches to life that he feels within himself; he is also in constant conflict with Melanie, as her need to be active seems to him—though she does not so intend it—to call in question the value of his work. They are devoted to each other; yet they are immensely different, and the tension within their marriage is not necessarily bad, though it might bring pain to the children, as it does to Colette. Paul feels, in fact, that "he and Melanie lived out their conflict—it was in a sense the very basis of their marriage, the rock which split them but on which they stood firm though there might be an abyss between" (205).

That marriage can absorb such tensions and that it is not a state of perpetual bliss even when it is deeply happy—such conclusions run like a minor theme throughout the novel. As the author deals with marriage in a realistic manner, it is seen as a state in which there can be no settled peace based on perfect communication between two people. Rather, marriage seems for both Paul and Melanie a constant mystery, a relationship that involves strain, doubt, and misunderstanding, and yet is good.

One of Melanie's most trying times is after Schmidt's first visit when Paul resumes his writing again with renewed energy and concentrates on it so exclusively that Melanie feels herself quite excluded from his thoughts. She tries to keep a sense of proportion, but she suffers. Momentarily, she begins to feel that she does not love Paul at all. "Marriage, she thought, was living with a stranger. Even now, after all these years, Paul was a stranger; never did she feel really safe, never quite off guard, never wholly accepted" (81). But she reasons her way to acceptance of the fact that "marriage is as much a matter of self-denial as self-fulfillment" (81), and that married people remain essentially solitary, though always together. Many years later, when Paul confides to Mlle Louvois his sense of failure and refrains from discussing it with Melanie, she again is grieved at being shut out from his life. This time Melanie's friend Simone says it is natural that, for a time, perhaps even for years, husband and wife might have little real communication. In fact, says Simone, " 'I can't imagine having perfect communion with anyone on the deepest level for more than moments now and then' " (169).

But if Melanie suffers because Paul seems to turn away from her, his own suffering is greater; for, until he writes his second book, his self-esteem is badly wounded. His sense of failure is acute; unable to write a book of philosophy that will sell, he stops speaking of wanting to write. He feels that he is a poor father, a poor husband, and a bad philosopher. It is interesting to see that Paul is saved from self-hatred, not directly by Melanie, but by Gerhart Schmidt, who himself suffers more than anyone in the book; for he is forced by his principles to leave both his family and his country.

In a sense, Schmidt's physical exile symbolizes the spiritual isolation of most of the characters in the book. The novel is remarkable not only for its sympathetic portrayal of many types of people—from Croll, the grumbling old gardener, to Simone, graceful and elegant, reclining on a chaise longue—but also for its concern with many kinds of suffering and separateness. Melanie, because she radiates love, suffers less than the others, most of whom are, in one way or another, exiles like Schmidt. Paul feels alone in his ivory tower; Françoise in the misery of adolescence finds life in the family at times unbearable; Pierre despises his father and mother, who grieve because he is so distant from them; Jacques, though he consents to marry Lou-Lou, wonders rather desperately what they will talk about when they live together. Colette and Solange, the "little ones," are still too encircled by the family to suffer much; but Colette in her bitter experience with Ado learns something of the world's grief.

Much of the isolation depicted in the novel arises from either lack of love or the wrong kind of love, such as Mlle Louvois' before she learned to be more selfless. Melanie and Schmidt are so influential on the others because they love and respect themselves and also love humanity at large. They are surprisingly alike; however, Schmidt shows his love for the world by dying, and Melanie by living. They both uphold and sustain not only Paul but the whole family because each in his own way refuses to despair. Each does what he *must* do with courage and faith.

Both Melanie and Schmidt seem to know instinctively something that Paul learns laboriously over many years—that it is possible to love humanity while seeing it as imperfect and in need of correction. Paul has always rebelled against the world's wrongs; but, until Schmidt's death, he has taken refuge in thought, feeling he must stay apart from the tumult to think. But in his second book he feels a sense of release; he realizes that for years he has longed for communication which his own aloofness had prevented. After hearing him read his book, his old professor congratulates him on a splendid work, saying that Paul was always a rebel, but now he has at last written with love. Now, he says, "you are still rebelling against this passionate age, determined to stand outside it, but your detachment has become positive instead of negative" (322). This positive detachment is easier for Melanie—she realizes she does not and should not possess her children—and for Schmidt it is enforced by his concern for humane values: neither family nor national loyalty can oppose, for him, his need to identify himself with those struggling for man's dignity and integrity.

But Paul sums up the theme of detachment in the novel. He feels, thinking of Melanie, that "It takes a long time, all one's life, to learn to love one person well—with enough distance, with enough humility" (237); and later, in his second book, he writes that men, out of their freedom and loneliness, must choose what they will do "with perfect love, which means perfect detachment." For God, he believes, is "the sum of our love when it learns complete detachment"(305). This detachment is what Mlle Louvois learns when she gives up her selfish interest in Paul; it is what gives Françoise a sense of joy when she relinquishes Jacques; it is this better understanding of God that Emile finds when he realizes the smothering nature of his love for his child, Pierre. The idea of "positive detachment" is dramatized in numerous ways throughout the book.

Many of the characters have moments of insight, a revelation of what life is or might be; but these moments are not stressed. With a sure understanding of reality, Miss Sarton presents in the novel a picture of much "daily life"—its small triumphs, persistent worries, and inevitable conflicts. The characters do grow and develop; the change is especially noticeable in Paul but is evident also in Melanie and the other main characters. But they change slowly, as in real life. Paul, remembering his intense joyousness when Colette was conceived, reflects that "Life was not lived at the point of intensity. . . . [It] might be conceived there, but it was sustained on another level, less pure, less violent, closer to earth, difficult, gradual, asking above all the ability to endure" (91).

There is a similar insight in Miss Sarton's poem "Humpty-Dumpty," where people are seen as able to recover from "great shocks" but find a slow attrition going on within themselves from many insignificant disappointments. The novel differs from the poem in that man is seen in *The Bridge of Years* as never really "overtaken" by the accumulation of griefs; instead, he endures. One of the "bridges" over the years is the toughness of the Duchesne family, its splendid courage and vitality. The reader is left with the feeling that no negative force in the world can permanently alter the resilience of the human spirit. As in another poem, "Take Anguish for Companion," Miss Sarton shows in *The Bridge of Years* the amazing power of people who can, like Paul, learn "positive detachment" and reach out, like Melanie, to help a suffering world.

III *Shadow of a Man* (1950)

The idea of detachment is given a quite different setting in Miss Sarton's next novel, *Shadow of a Man*, which begins and ends in New England. But the Old World strongly influences the new, and a large portion of the book shows the hero, Francis Chabrier, in Paris. The novel is the story of his coming to maturity, and what he learns from Europe and from his affair with a Parisian woman is the most important element in his finding himself and his purpose in life.

In Part I the reader is caught up in the shock that comes to the

family on the sudden death of Francis' mother, Persis Chabrier
Bradford. Mrs. Bradford had been so vital, so influential on those
who knew her, that none of her friends or family can take her
death lightly. Her second husband, Alan Bradford, feels stricken
and lifeless himself; and both he and Francis are uncomfortable
without Persis' "mediating presence" (3). For Francis has never
accepted Alan; he has resented or merely tolerated him from the
time his mother married again when Francis was fourteen. He is
now a graduate student at Harvard, uncertain of his career,
prickly and on the defensive with relatives who feel that by age
twenty-six he should have decided something about his future.

Francis is insecure partly because he is only half-American;
some of his loyalty is to his French father, Pierre Chabrier, who,
he feels, is not enough respected by the Boston relatives. Partly he
has always felt dwarfed by his brilliant mother, who had been so
anxious not to be possessive that she left him in doubt as to her
real love for him. Persis Bradford had in no way been a usual
mother, "no maker of pies, dispenser of comforts. . . ." Instead,
she had expected much of him: "At moments of crisis she had
left her son alone, demanded his best at all times, taken him seriously always, which meant fighting him every inch of the way,
testing his mind against her own, forcing him to grow to meet her"
(17).

The result is, now that she is dead, Francis feels he can never
know what she really thought of him, but that he must fulfill her
great hopes for him. But he also wants to be a person in his own
right, independent of her and above all of what seems to him
the narrow atmosphere of Boston. Except for his Aunt Alison, who
shows him her affection, he feels "the poverty of relationship"
(78) in New Englanders. But he shies away from emotional involvement with Ann Winthrop, whom he has known since childhood; she is in love with him and finds his apparent lack of emotion distressing. On a walk that they take just after Persis' death,
he says that he will go to Paris in the summer, as he had intended
to do with his mother; and there perhaps he may become himself.
When Ann replies, in a kind of panic, that perhaps he will fall in
love in Paris, he answers "with heavy irony" that he does not
"seem to be capable of that almost universal emotion . . ." (55).
She must face the bleak prospect of a summer without Francis and
his mother, and she tries not to show her hurt and disappointment.

Francis, Alan, and Ann are not the only ones to be deeply grieved and upset by Persis' sudden death. There is also Saul Wiseman, Francis' college friend who flies from Detroit to attend the funeral and to help Francis in this difficult time. Saul has known Mrs. Bradford as a wonderful, understanding friend who comforted him when his own mother died; now he feels the double force of both deaths and a sense of terrible isolation.

After the funeral, Francis and Alan come to know each other a bit better; and the tension between them is brought into the open. Each now feels not chiefly hostility but pity. Francis, realizing that Alan had deeply loved his mother and that she had not loved him in the same way, is sorry; and Alan pities Francis because he understands the "binding and difficult" nature of the relationship between parents and children (90).

In Part II, Francis goes to Paris and meets his mother's old friend, Solange Bernard, "in whose single person he was seeking his father and his mother, his childhood and himself" (109). After his first visit to her, he is "filled with an immense unreasoning happiness" (123); though she is so much older than he, he has fallen in love. To her, their affair begins to seem inevitable. Her love for him is never so intense as his; but, starting with a tenderness for him because of Persis, Solange ends by loving him for himself—his impetuousity, his ardor that makes her feel young again. When he has become Solange's lover, Francis is at last independent of his mother. His joy in sexual love is like religious fervor; and, because Solange brings him so much new awareness, he feels, at the height of their affair, that he must somehow "give back to life" some of his happiness; and he decides that he will become a teacher. On that very night, Solange begins to withdraw from him; for she feels that so much of her life is behind her, and so much of his ahead, that he must now make his own way without her. But, though she has "opened the door into his real life" (177), he is crushed, angry, and bewildered by her rejection. She, though, is grieved for him even as she rejects him; and her suffering *with* him helps him to see the pain and difficulty of love.

A help to both of them is the arrival of Alan for a holiday visit. To Solange, he seems already like an old friend; and, in their discussion of Francis, Alan says that "someone had to hurt him to bring him alive" (224). He feels that Francis will eventually be grateful to her; for Alan believes that "only the wounded eye sees"

(225). In the last weeks in Paris, Solange and Francis achieve a kind of peace. Francis is not happy but is resolved to go back to America with Alan, for he has been offered a teaching job in a small college in Iowa; and, "enclosed in a brilliant solitariness," he tells Solange goodbye (244).

Part III deals with their return to Boston in August. Later, in Maine, Francis finds the other Boston relatives and friends who go there each summer. He also finds Ann, who seems amazingly happy and free—not "pinched" and grieving as when he left. He realizes that he is in love with her; and, after some hesitation (because it seems disloyal to Solange), he asks her to marry him. Ann, who still loves him, understands that what Solange did for Francis was to open him to a more lasting love, "something deeper than romantic" (301). She tells him that Solange "will be like poetry to you always . . . but I'll be . . . bread and bed and house and home" (302). For his part, Francis now feels content not to be highly exceptional as in his restless uncertainty he had hoped to be. He has accepted the fact that "gods cast long shadows" and that it is "dangerous to be so free" as gods are. Instead, he wants human responsibility, and he will cast a "plain human shadow . . . the shadow of a man" (302).

This story of the coming-of-age of a young man is interesting not only for itself but in its relation to Miss Sarton's preceding novels and poetry. Some of the same themes are here—passion, detachment, the conflict between generations, and the pain of living in two worlds and feeling at home in neither. But this last theme is not strongly stressed. Francis is tense and uneasy in the first part of the book, but the reason is as much his feeling overshadowed by his brilliant mother as his knowledge that he does not fully "belong" in America. And a great part of his arriving at maturity comes from his understanding, while in France, of how the New World can be "nourished" by the Old. In contrast to Saul, who is so entranced by European culture that he remains in Paris instead of returning with his friend, Francis prefers to live in America where everything is just beginning. His delight in Paris is equalled by his new appreciation of America as a place of "immense possibility." He says once that " 'Americans have everything except souls' " (170), and his ambition is to use his new insight into life and people, his new appreciation of beauty to help civilize the students he will teach.

The Boston setting of the novel is vividly portrayed by details that evoke the spirit of the people as well as the place. The reader sees the big house on Mount Vernon Street; the twin beds in the bedroom of Persis and Alan, with the framed picture of Pierre Chabrier on a table between them; the street on a winter night, "the halo of light around the street lamp and the thick-falling snow, and one light high up in the house opposite" (100); Aunt Alison's untidy apartment "with its old velvet sofa covered with clippings and liberal journals, its rows of books on economics and history, the photographs of Tom Mooney, Sacco and Van-zetti, Jaurès . . ." (28). In general, Bostonians are shown as frugal, highly idealistic and good, but as shy in the presence of emotion. At the funeral, Saul finds himself wondering if he really believes in God; and his attitude, sitting with his head in his hands, is "so unexpectedly devout that it disturbed the old gentle-man on his right." For "It was not usual here to assume such attitudes; a discreet bowing of the head, arms folded, seemed more appropriate to the dignity of man and the Majesty to whom he appeals" (61).

The contrast between the physical and psychological cold of Boston that winter and the beauty of Paris in early summer makes Francis feel liberated. Even before he meets Solange he is en-tranced by the spaces and colors, the "blue and white and gold and green, all soft and shining" of the place he had not seen for so many years. All the passages describing Paris are written with lyrical beauty. When Francis arrives, the city is "veiled in a hya-cinthine light, damp that never became rain, but stayed suspended over lavender streets . . ." (107). Such beauty, enhanced when he falls in love, seems a symbol of his awareness of what Europe offers to America.

His return home with Alan is a test of his new insight, for they arrive in the middle of searing August heat. The heavy, dank atmosphere of downtown Boston, the shriveled trees, the stale smell of the closed-up house—all are in sharp contrast to the beauty he has left. But in his mother's room, while he is lying on the floor listening to a Mozart concerto, he feels the pattern of his life emerging with the intricate passages of the music. As his mother had blended the old and new worlds, he also can. And later, the cold, bracing air of Maine, where he meets Ann, is appropriate for his new resolution. So the author uses scenery, the atmosphere of Europe and America, to reinforce moods and ideas.

It is its themes and its evocation of places that are the strength of the novel. Its plot is weakened by the "happy-ever-after" ending which seems, despite the author's efforts to explain it, rather forced. It is quite believable that Francis should be able to respond to Ann for the first time, once he has had another experience of love; but the actual engagement, complete with a diamond brooch left by Persis for Ann at her marriage, is less convincing than a subtler ending would have been. Francis' certainty about his career, with simply the possibility of marriage with Ann, might have indicated the kind of joy most likely in the real world.

The diamond brooch does, however, serve to remind the reader of the unity achieved in the novel through the character of Persis. Though she is shown only through the other persons in the story, her power is such that she is never forgotten, either by them or by the reader. Her death clarifies Alan's relationship not only to Francis but to old Mrs. Bradford, his mother; it brings new peace to Alan and acts as a spur to Francis, urging him to do what her well-concealed love never did—to find out the meaning of his life; and it helps, through Solange, Francis and Saul, to bring the old world closer to the new.

As in *The Bridge of Years*, this novel shows the author's keen awareness of the suffering of women—especially that caused by love. Ann must carefully conceal her pain on hearing Francis say that he has "meant to" fall in love with her but has not: "Her face felt completely frozen with the effort to be dispassionate" (57). And Solange, after she has ended the affair with Francis, resents his having broken into her "small reserve of peace and joy" with his shattering demands. She knows that emotion will be for him a "motor force" which will help him to think and will "light up his whole world," but love is not like that for women. She wonders, "Does he have any idea . . . how different love is to a woman, what a price women pay for love, rooted as it is deep inside them, not a mere release of excess energy, but something to be contained, received, and always involving human responsibility? She did not want to be responsible for Francis" (201).

What Francis does not realize (and what Solange may be only partly aware of) is that he falls in love with an imaginary person.

The following passage, showing something of the nature of passion, is typical of Miss Sarton's unobtrusive but wise comments on love: "There was a whole night and half a day before he would see her. Already behind the real figure an intangible figure, the figure of his imagination, was forming itself, the secret person the lover creates who is perhaps not there at all, the person the lover creates out of his own need and to his own dimension" (136). The same would apply to Mark in his love for Georgia (*The Single Hound*) and Françoise in hers for Jacques in *The Bridge of Years*.

As in the earlier novels, a sharp distinction is also made in *Shadow of a Man* between love and passion. Just as passion gives to Mark a new energy and power, so to Francis it gives a feeling that the world is for the first time open to him. But this fierce energy is not love, which always implies tenderness and "real communion" of the mind and spirit as well as of the body. Solange knows "that passion is a poison and always someone dies of it, someone is cruelly hurt" (157). And Francis, on the night when Solange withdraws from him, finds that pure delight has turned into a "frightful and exhausting" sexual battle (178). For the first time, he is aware "of the tragic undercurrent of all passion that can lead nowhere but back into itself. . . ." Because of their difference in age, he and Solange will never marry or have a child. Their passion "cannot in the end be used, be translated back into life, a shared life where love will open again all the doors that this raging desire to possess and to be possessed has closed" (179). His love for Ann, on the other hand, does not mean a battle. He calls it "dear love, not terrible love" (302); and he means that it is not, at least at the moment, passion at all. With Ann he may, in the end, have both passion and real love.

An equally important theme, as in Miss Sarton's poetry and the first two novels, is that of detachment. One of the most beautiful scenes in *Shadow of a Man* occurs at the end of Part I, where Alan comes to see that, because death has taken Persis from him, he at last possesses her. His love for her had far exceeded hers for him, so that as long as she lived he felt always unsatisfied. Now, four days after her death, all is different: "Outside the snow fell, the silence fell and here in his bed Alan realized that the only wall which had remained to keep Persis and him apart was gone forever—that insurmountable wall of his passion for her. Now that she was dead, he possessed her at last, because he was free. Peace and love flowed in and soon Alan slept" (103).

Persis herself had the rare quality of detachment, which, the author makes clear, is only possible to those who are capable of intense feeling. Talking to Francis of his mother, Solange says, "Only really passionate people know anything about detachment . . . because they are forced to learn it or to die; no one comes willingly to detachment" (138). Certainly, Francis himself comes to it unwillingly through Solange's withdrawal; but he learns a great deal by it. Only when he has been forced to give up Solange does he understand his mother and see her clearly, "free from all his own feeling about her, free to be herself for him, and apart from him, as if a cloud had been dispersed between them" (199).

Ann, too, learns detachment when Francis shows that he does not care for her. She is forced to "die away" from him, really give him up; then, miraculously, she feels free for the first time and is thus more attractive to him when he returns from Paris. Here is still a further instance of the truth of the refrain in Miss Sarton's poem, "O Saisons! O Châteaux!": "We only keep what we lose."

The maturity that Francis is developing by the end of the novel is similar to that attained by Mark Taylor and Françoise Duchesne; for all of these characters, detachment is achieved in relationship to one person. For Paul Duchesne it is perhaps something deeper, as it is related to all of life and affects his attitude toward humanity as a whole. But for Paul detachment is "positive"—it includes a going forward to meet the world. For Francis, it means a separation painful but necessary, one of the hardest things for the young to learn.

VIII   *A Shower of Summer Days* (1952)

In her next novel, *A Shower of Summer Days,* Miss Sarton was again concerned with a young person who learns to cope with suffering; and, as in *Shadow of a Man,* the plot turns partly on the confrontation of the Old World and the New. But this novel has as characters not only people but also a house: Dene's Court, the Irish country house where many generations of Denes have lived, has a distinct personality of its own. It influences both its owners, who return to it after an absence of thirty years, and Sally, the young American who comes to it for the first time.

Miss Sarton spoke, in a lecture at Scripps College, of the origin

of *A Shower of Summer Days*. The novel began as a "psychic disturbance" within her after she had stayed for a few days at Elizabeth Bowen's house in Cork County, Ireland. Her description of
the experience and its result is interesting to those who wonder
how a novel begins:

> My room was a corner room, with four large windows; I remem-
> ber Lowestoft bowls full of roses on small tables, silver candle-
> sticks, a great red satin puff on the bed. But there was no desk.
> The first thing a writer does when he walks into a room is to
> look for a desk, and in a few minutes I had moved furniture
> around, taken a mirror, a bowl of roses, and the candlesticks off
> one of the tables, and pulled it over to the east window. I worked
> very happily there for days. But after I left, I found that I was
> troubled. Apparently in disturbing the ancient and noble order
> of a room in this great seventeenth century house, I had com-
> mitted an outrage . . . upon the beautiful form of a house which
> in itself had a strong personality.[3]

For about a year following, she says that she was haunted by the
house and its power; and, in trying to answer the question as to
why it had so disturbed her, she wrote the novel. She feels that
most novels begin with questions which sometimes lie dormant in
the subconscious for a long time before they are recognized as
fertile ideas for a novel. In fact, Miss Sarton believes that "the
only possible reason for engaging in the hard labor of writing a
novel, is that one is bothered by something one needs to understand, and can come to understand only, as the psychiatrists would
say, 'by acting out' through the characters in the imagined situation." [4]

The novel begins with the house; Violet and Charles Gordon
are returning to Violet's old home after thirty years in Burma.
Before they appear on the scene, the reader sees the house through
the eyes of Annie Ryan, the old woman who has worked for the
Denes in Violet's childhood. After Annie receives letters and a
telephone call asking her to open the house, she enlists the aid
of Maire, a sixteen-year-old relative; and they begin cleaning and
airing all the rooms. While they work, Annie tells Maire the history of Dene's Court; as she talks, "processions of summers rose
up and faded away; carriages gave way to motor cars . . . croquet
parties came and went; Jonas Oliver Dene and his wife Elisabeth

(Violet's grandparents) seemed always to be alighting from a drive and standing on the terrace steps waving at someone" (8).

Annie's love for the house and her loyalty to all its occupants set the mood of nostalgia that dominates the first part of the book; for Violet, too, is remembering the past. In the hotel in Dublin and after she and Charles arrive, she remembers both the happy and the painful times of her girlhood and feels apprehension about the future: will she and Charles find themselves diminished by the weight of tradition and all the intense life that had been lived at Dene's Court? One of Violet's most painful memories is of her sister Barbie, who had always, as they were growing up, felt overshadowed by Violet's beauty. Her older sister's very existence seemed to Barbie a threat, for she was vivacious but not beautiful; and she had to wear Violet's cast-off clothes, and on one occasion when she had fallen in love, the young man had danced one evening with Violet and had lost interest in Barbie. Violet herself had not wanted to hurt her sister, but she had been "self-intoxicated, needing to feel her power, flirting unconsciously and consciously every moment of the day, expecting homage as a princess expects it, taking it as her due" (57). Ever since their girlhood, long after Barbie had married and gone with her husband to America, Violet has felt guilty.

Now, soon after her return to Dene's Court, Violet receives a letter from Barbie, asking if she might send her daughter Sally for a visit, so that she will forget her infatuation with Ian, an American actor. Knowing that it will not be an easy situation, for Sally does not want to come, Violet nevertheless feels she cannot refuse her sister anything. She and Charles wait with mounting suspense for Sally's arrival. When Charles brings Sally from the Shannon airport in the late afternoon of a June day, she, looking up at "the high bleak stone face of the house" (69) is amazed at the vastness of it; it seems to her like a prison, and in her bewilderment and exhaustion she falls on the stone stairs of the entrance instead of running up them. Inside, she is no more at ease: she feels she is losing "her power to be herself" (70), that in the immense rooms she is small and insignificant. Also, resenting the fact that here she is expected to forget Ian, she determines to ignore the beauty and dignity of the house and to resist the charm of her aunt and uncle.

In order to "remain intact" (77), Sally disturbs the order of her room by moving furniture and by strewing her clothes and books about; she wears blue jeans and plays loud, yawping jazz on her portable radio. Violet feels that the house "rejected this so violently that the very walls sent it back, echoing" (78). Sally feels too that the room rejects the music, but jazz has been "the climate of her relationship with Ian" (88), and she must hold on to her memory of him, especially as his letters are unsatisfactory and do nothing to make him seem closer. But gradually, after trying in many ways to disrupt the rhythm of life in the house and to keep Violet and Charles at bay, Sally becomes more and more curious about her aunt and uncle—their being still so much in love and so at home in surroundings that are to her difficult and overwhelming.

Though she decides that they are "useless people like the people of Chekhov" (113), she finds herself drawn into their world almost against her will. She especially admires her aunt for her beauty and poise, and she ends by being a little in love with Violet. As the feeling increases, she changes her ways; she tidies her room, wears dresses instead of jeans, and builds up a fantasy in which every word and look of Violet's is of enormous significance. Relationships among the three become strained during a period of rainy weather when they cannot often get out of the house. Charles flirts with Sally, who responds so that Violet will not guess the depth of her feeling for herself. But Violet, who knows and is worried because Sally seems to be silently asking something she cannot give, becomes alarmed also at the undercurrent of seriousness in Charles's flirtation. She has known of many of her husband's brief love affairs and made no comment, but this one must not be allowed to develop. When she warns Sally of what is happening to Charles, Sally, who had taken Charles's attentions only with gratitude because they made her feel accepted and part of the life of the house, is shocked and hurt. She avoids her uncle as much as possible.

But Sally also realizes, after Violet's revelation, just what has been happening to her. She has "all the time been in love not only with Violet but with her marriage, with Charles and Violet as an entity" (154); and it is "the charm of their life together against which her relation with Ian was slowly disintegrating . . ." (154). She sees that she must make her own life, not "take something already created" (167). But she now belongs neither to Dene's

Court nor to the world of Ian; she feels free but very much alone. At this crucial point, she receives a letter from Ian, asking if he may fly to Ireland for a week-end visit with them. Longing for some certainty and reassurance, she writes to tell him to come before consulting her aunt or her uncle. Each of them is at first astonished and hurt, feeling too that Ian's being allowed to come is a betrayal of Barbie's trust. But Violet understands Sally's lost feeling and uncertainty about her future. Charles, when he hears the news, is furious; after an angry scene, which Sally runs away from in distress, Violet tells her husband that she understands why he is upset—that he is half in love with Sally. To his real surprise, he sees that this has been the truth; Violet has understood it before he had. He is shocked by "what the summer madness had almost led him into . . ." (178).

When Ian arrives—dapper, impeccably dressed, and very sure of himself—Sally waits in great suspense for some demonstration of his love. But he does not, as she had half expected, ask her to marry him; he does not even kiss her except in a polite way. Instead, he tells her that he plans to go to Hollywood for two years. When he seems more interested in Violet and Dene's Court than in Sally, all are puzzled about why he has come. On the second day of his visit, when he seeks out Violet while she is arranging the flowers, she asks him directly if he is in love with Sally. He says that he had thought he was; now, seeing her in the house, he is not sure. Later, to Sally, who is driven by her suffering to ask him the same question, he answers that he feels incapable of love. Soon after this episode, when they all go for a drive, Sally shows a strange exhilaration; her despair acts as a liberating force for a while, though she knows that pain will come later. She confides to Charles, who now feels only fatherly affection for her, that all is over with her and Ian and that she feels " 'so queer, like an orphan—or a leper' " (217). Later, when they return to the house, she runs to the great empty ballroom but resists the impulse to give way to tears again. She determines that she can only learn to be "human" if she can control her emotions. She sees Ian as someone not quite human, whom she had blindly worshipped.

Ian confesses to Violet, in two of his intimate talks that he insists on having, that his real reason for coming was curiosity about her. Sally's letters had depicted her as irresistibly charming; and, though he had at first been jealous, he ended by having to come

to see Violet for himself. Violet realizes, sadly, that the old pattern
has repeated itself. She has done to Sally what she used to do to
Barbie and has done to others all her life—her beauty and her
charm have attracted someone without her knowing or wanting
it. She feels guilty, as always, because it seems to her she must
have subconsciously tried to attract: " 'In my heart of hearts, I
suppose I want to be loved. You only call out of people what you
want to call out. It doesn't just happen. That's the guilt . . .' "
(235).

When Ian leaves the next morning, Sally asks Violet to go with
him and Charles, but she herself wants to remain at the house.
After they have gone, she asks Annie for a pair of golves and goes
out to the stable to clear out the nettles around it. To do so is a
way of asserting her identity as a person who is free and who is
beginning at last to create her own life.

This summary of the plot gives little indication of the complexity and subtlety of *Shower of Summer Days*. Not a great deal
"happens" in the usual sense. But the atmosphere, the characterization, and the theme work together to create a suspense not
dependent on physical action. Since Dene's Court dominates the
idea of the novel, the action takes place there. A walk that Violet
and Sally have to the village is only a "brief excursion" (159), and
both it and the drive that all four characters take on the weekend
of Ian's visit are climaxed by their approach to the house on their
return.

The effect of the house on all their emotions is made clear by
numerous descriptions of its façade, which rises like a forbidding
or reassuring presence. And they are aware not only of its vastness—the great, high-ceilinged rooms, the long corridors, the "big
naked windows" (24)—but also of its austere charm, and the softer
beauty around it setting it in relief: the "great bowl of hills" (104)
in the distance, the sweep of rolling lawn and the walled garden
with its flowers, and the constantly changing weather always apparent through the great windows. Sally, watching her aunt ar-
range flowers in the morning, is startled by darkness: "At this
moment clouds must have swept over the sun for the room was
suddenly dark, so dark that it was hard to see. Sally had never
been in a house where the outside weather was so important, and
as the outside weather never remained the same for more than a

few hours, this too added to her feeling of suspense, of unreality. Now heavy straight rain poured down" (92).

Through sense images, the atmosphere of Dene's Court, past and present, is made real. Violet recalls a dance held in the house on a July evening, "the outer green dark reflected in the long mirrors, with points of candle flame like lights coming up through water flaring through them, and roses transformed into subaqueous flowers" (60). On the morning when she and Charles take Sally to pick wild strawberries, she remembers other hot days in her childhood when the sun had beat down and when the larks had twittered high in the sky. The following passage, describing the bedroom on a moonlit night, uses sounds and images as in a poem:

> . . . now outside the air was milky white, and as Violet and Charles lay in bed and got accustomed to the dark, it seemed to grow brighter and brighter; they could see the wide path across the foot of the bed and against the sharp white of the closed door. A light cool wind stirred the curtains. All seemed so clear and wide-open . . . that they were drawn irresistibly to the windows to look out, to look down on the side of the real lawn, at the still flower beds, at the roses gone black in the moonlight and the blue-white petunias (54).

With the same economy that limits the novel to one rich evocative place, Miss Sarton concentrates on four characters. The three minor characters are the servants: Cammaert the gardener and Annie the cook show the continuity of life in the house since they remember its days of grandeur; and the girl Maire represents one more person who admires and secretly adores Violet. The main characters, the center around which the three servants move, are depicted in such careful detail that the reader is left feeling he has known them a long time: Violet with her sophistication, her beauty, her burden of guilt that she does not dwell upon but never quite forgets; Charles, who prefers action to speech, likes to tease, and is called an "innocent" because he has no subterfuge; Ian, who for all his smooth charm is terribly vulnerable and has not yet learned how to live or love; and, above all, Sally—intense, demanding, lovable, who will be greatly hurt by life because of the passion with which she gives herself to it. She has traits in common with Mark in *The Single Hound* and with Francis in

Shadow of a Man; but she is also quite different, entirely herself. Along with her intensity, she has great common sense. Like Melanie in *Bridge of Years,* she speaks severely to herself and will not allow Ian's withdrawal to crush her. Like Francis, she wants to become "more human." When she finally realizes that she has been attached to Ian like a pagan worshiper before a "little golden idol," she reflects: "We have to find the way to be human without disintegrating into messy little feelings" (225).

As in a play by Chekhov, the action of the novel is inward: what the four characters think and feel is dominant. Sally's rather patronizing thought that her aunt and uncle are Chekhovian, which is later voiced by Ian, does more than simply "place" Violet and Charles in an era. Instead, it suggests the tone of the whole story—a concern for people caught in the perplexities of the human situation. All four individuals are presented with compassion; and they seem not only themselves but representatives of all humanity. Where Sally and Ian show the uncertainty and honesty of questioning youth, Violet and Charles have the mature confidence which is always tinged with the fear of old age and waning powers.

As in *The Bridge of Years,* marriage is portrayed as anything but settled and secure. Violet and Charles are still very much in love, but their very passion keeps them in a state of peril. Violet is aware of this situation; but, like Melanie, she knows that love within marriage must ebb and flow; the relationship is always "demanding, disappointing, ecstatic" (29). But Violet also feels "a kind of terror and despair" as she realizes that Charles's love for her is based more on physical attraction than on understanding. They have never really been friends. She has for many years tolerated his occasional lack of faithfulness because she knows that he will always return to her; but what, she wonders, may happen when he no longer finds her attractive? This unromantic view of marriage is typical of the Realism of the novel that sees Sally's immature love creating a fantasy about both Violet and Ian.

The need for real love—not the ecstasy of passion, but something nearer to respect—is one of the novel's basic themes; and all the characters seek reassurance and the steadying force of love. All of them are touchingly unsure of themselves, even Violet, who seems to the young people the epitome of self-confidence. Charles flirts with Sally because her response makes him feel young and dashing again. Ian seeks out Violet for confidential talks because he longs for her approval; he wants her to understand why he is giving up Sally, and perhaps he also subconsciously hopes he will gain from Violet a knowledge of how to love. One of the book's most interesting ironies is the fact that Violet, on whom the love and admiration of the other three center, is not lifted by their adoration to any height. She feels at times both fear and guilt. The author is saying that, no matter what the façade, underneath it all people need desperately to be reassured about their own worth.

All the main characters grow and change, but in Sally the growth is greatest. She sees that people need to be loved to be given an identity. She understands, the more keenly because of her suffering, that Violet and Ian alike call forth love from others "not because they needed love as she did so desperately, but because they needed to be given back to themselves, an entirely other thing" (200). She wonders despairingly whether she can ever become lovable: Ian no longer loves her, and she therefore is losing some essence of herself. Violet too realizes, perhaps not quite so clearly, that in a strange way she "finds" herself when she sees the expected admiration in the eyes of Sally, Ian, and even Maire. But Sally is struggling to attain this very "self" and cries out, " 'How am I ever to get to be like Aunt Violet if nobody loves me whom I can love?' " (210).

In her search for identity and for the meaning of life, Sally is helped not so much by any one person as by the house. In the beginning it seems her enemy, but she comes to regard it as a challenge. Where it is at first a bewildering puzzle, this "big house set down in the midst of the country" (110) representing only a musty tradition, it assumes significance. Perhaps because the house "was built to maintain, to endure, built in danger and on belief," it gives her courage (173). By the time Ian arrives, she has been so affected by the staunch spirit the house seems to have that she feels that it protects her from fear—the fear of what Ian will say. She now has something he will not understand, for Ian "could not possibly imagine what majesty of youth and age, and what judgment would stand on the terrace to greet him, she with the house behind her and its great cold eyes staring out behind hers" (183).

But if the house is, to both Sally and Violet, a protection, and "a form for the chaotic hours, the changes of time and feeling" (225), it also at times seem to accuse them, to ask more than they can give. Against its ancient stalwartness, people seem frail and transitory. Even Charles, on his arrival, feels too exposed in the house—"from within, the freight of memories; from without, the inescapable invading light of dark, sun or rain . . ." (24). Violet wonders, "Do we have enough life in us . . . to fill these spaces? To withstand all this?" (20). All the characters, especially Sally, feel that so much life has been experienced in the house in the past, so much has been endured, that they ought to live with greater faith and fortitude. So the influence of the past is constantly, in this novel, extending to the present. And all that the house stands for helps Sally to gain the detachment necessary to make a free and significant life. Like Mark Taylor and Francis Chabrier, she matures when she learns to renounce. What she has to surrender is not only Ian and her fantasy of his love but also her wish to enter the private world of Violet and Charles. Her feeling about them would become true perhaps if she could come to look at them without wishing either to possess or to be possessed by what they had (167). She must find her own meaning in life. Her first action after Ian leaves for America is to begin to clear away nettles; and the symbolism of this act recalls to a reader of Miss Sarton's early volume of poetry, *Inner Landscape,* one sonnet that uses a similar image, the "prickly paradise" that is the actual fulfillment of a romantic dream. The end of *Shower of Summer Days* seems inevitable and right. Sally's course in the future will not be easy; but she finds, as perhaps her mother had intended, a new certainty, a better understanding of herself.

So in this novel, as in *Shadow of a Man,* the Old World provides a refuge and a painful kind of healing power for the New World. But it is not Sally who stands as a symbol of America, so much as Ian, for Ian, who has not yet found himself, hides his uncertainty under a bland assertion of superiority. He is too well dressed, too clean, too smooth to seem at first quite human. He wants to become a movie star, the kind of person most responsible for stereotyped ideas about Americans. But he has great curiosity about Violet, and he begins to learn something. Violet, with her greater age and experience, symbolizes the Old World. Because she is more complex and subtle than Sally, Ian breaks his half-engagement. In herself, Violet feels protective and responsible toward the young people; but she also feels guilt for what she has done to people in the past.

But such symbolism, interesting and provocative as it is, is not the chief strength of the novel. It lies, rather, in the skillful interweaving of the lives and emotions of four people so as to show them all fixed in time and place and yet somehow transcending these limitations. Like Dene's Court, the characters suggest much more than what at first is seen; they are figures in a universal story.

CHAPTER 4

The Later Novels: Communion

IN THE second group of Miss Sarton's novels, published before *Kinds of Love* (1970), the need for communion is dominant. The passionate individual who so often appeared in the early novels is still prominent in the second group, but now his need is not so much for the ordering of his own inner chaos as for dealing somehow with chaos in the world. To some extent, of course, the attempt to bring order into both the inner and the outer realm is the same process; personal passion must be sublimated and become concern for the outer world. But the emphasis in the second group of novels is not so much on a necessary detachment as on the need described in the author's poem, "Innumerable Friend," to "Take the immense dangerous leap to understand, / Build an invisible bridge from mind to mind. . . ." [1]

I *Faithful Are the Wounds* (1955)

In *Faithful Are the Wounds,* set in Cambridge and Boston, the main character is Edward Cavan, a brilliant professor of American literature at Harvard. Beginning with the news of his suicide, the narrative moves backward in time to show how his family and his childhood help to explain him, and then forward, so that, through the reactions of his shocked and grieving friends, the reader understands why Cavan threw himself under a train. The era is during the national hysteria of the McCarthy investigations, which is just beginning (the germ of the book was, in fact, the suicide of Professor F. O. Matthiessen); but, in its wider implications, the novel moves beyond the immediate circumstances to the author's conviction that the true intellectual must be concerned not only with his own field of study but with the great political issues of his time.

The mood of tension that pervades the entire book is established in the first episode when Cavan's sister, Isabel Ferrier, receives a telephone call about her brother's death. Ever since they were children, Isabel has worried about Edward. Even now, living in California and married to a successful surgeon, she has been deeply troubled by Edward's extremism in politics, his attitude of angry denunciation of the middle-class values that she and her husband hold. When she hears of his suicide, she feels she has somehow always known it would happen—some frightful violence that she has been dreading all these years is the inevitable outcome of Edward's being so different and so difficult. Now she must leave immediately for Boston, and the departure from her safe, uneventful life is painful.

After the Prologue that shows Isabel at home and on her way to the East, the story moves to a week earlier and to the events that immediately preceded the suicide. George Hastings, a graduate student who greatly admires Cavan, finishes the outline of his doctoral dissertation and in mood of exaltation goes to find Cavan. He cannot, as he has planned, ask Cavan to dinner, for the moment is not right, but they have coffee together; George realizes that Cavan is deeply troubled by the state of the world— the fear that is creeping into many areas of life, as shown specifically in the firing of professors with liberal ideas.

The reader next sees Cavan attending, with his old friend Grace Kimlock, a meeting of the Civil Liberties Union. On hearing a request that their branch of the organization give a statement of non-Communist involvement, Cavan and Grace protest vigorously; but Professor Damon Phillips, another member of long standing, speaks in favor of the statement. Cavan leaves the meeting and breaks off with Phillips. Grace, who all her life has fought for political freedom and the rights of minorities, is terribly upset. But neither she nor Cavan's other elderly friend, Orlando Fosca, can bring any real comfort to him. Fosca, when Edward comes to see him, has the impression that the "real Edward" is imprisoned inside this stranger who sits nervous, tense, and unable to speak of what is troubling him.

But Cavan carries on with his work at the university. George brings Pen Wallace, the girl he hopes to marry, to a meeting of Cavan's seminar, and she is impressed by his penetration and honesty as a scholar but also with his seeming to be terribly vulnerable. After the seminar, Cavan goes to see Ivan Goldberg, the head of his department, to ask him to lead a committee of protest against the firing of a midwestern professor who had campaigned for the liberal Henry Wallace, the Progressive party candidate for president. Goldberg refuses; he believes that professors should concern themselves with their teaching and scholarly work and not meddle in politics; to him Edward's feeling of responsibility for others is "morbid." When Edward tries to convince him that the firing of Professor Lode is " 'the opening wedge in a fight against the intellectuals as subversives not only for political reasons but because they're intellectuals,' " he fails (106). Later, when he goes for a walk with Grace, she feels powerless to lift the weight of his depression.

Meanwhile, Julia Phillips, Damon's wife, with whom Edward has felt an affinity, has invited him to dinner in an effort to repair the broken friendship. Though Edward comes and though they talk frankly of their disagreement, he cannot accept Damon's compromising position; and he tells them both goodbye. Damon, who is always inwardly unsure of himself, wonders if he might, after all, be wrong. Julia is distressed to realize that their love and friendship for Edward cannot prevent his breaking away. Her cry, " 'Why can't love help?' " (134) expresses also the bewilderment of his other friends, when they learn that Cavan has killed himself.

Part II shows first the reactions of the various friends and associates when they know that Cavan is dead. George Hastings, dumb with grief, is appalled at his own self-interest, for his first reaction on hearing the news was to remember that Cavan had promised to help him get an instructorship at Harvard. Julia is more stricken than Damon, who temporarily puts aside his remorse by talking to students about Edward's value as a dissenter in society. Ivan Goldberg, who takes over Edward's seminar, is so filled with guilt and grief that he cannot bring himself to mention Cavan's name when he meets the students—and they think him heartless. Fosca, who has had the painful task of identifying the body, comforts Grace by saying that the dead reveal the essence of themselves and so sustain the living.

When Damon and Julia meet Isabel at the airport, she finds some relief for her pent-up feelings by talking with them about her brother. The next day Isabel meets the clergyman who will conduct the funeral and has lunch with Ivan Goldberg; at the Phillipses' house, where she meets Grace and Fosca, she talks again about Edward. None of them know just why he took his life, but they all find themselves having to re-examine their own beliefs. To Isabel, who has never before known university people, this world is alien; but she begins gradually to understand something of the spiritual conflict that drove Edward to suicide.

Alone in Edward's apartment, she thinks of how as a child he had been forced to witness his mother's suffering in her inharmonious marriage, and she sees the pattern repeated in his adulthood, when he was again a helpless witness who was aware of injustice and selfishness but unable to help. A similar revelation as to Edward's dilemma comes to George Hastings when he and Pen talk about the tragedy; and afterward when she leaves—too quickly as always—he feels his old frustration at never being able to communicate freely with her; his own deep feeling for her always keeps him too tense. This situation, he sees, may be, on a small scale, like the one that Cavan faced.

The Epilogue describes a senatorial investigation five years later. Damon Phillips has been accused of Communist sympathies and must stand trial. George and Pen, who are now married, drive Grace to the courthouse. Under the too-smooth questioning of the committee, Damon shows that he is no longer a compromiser; when asked abut his association with Edward Cavan, who is accused of having been a Communist, Damon defends himself and Edward as free, responsible citizens. When Damon refuses to give the names of other accused friends, he is held in contempt of Congress. Grace, who has been holding back her anger, cries aloud, " 'Disgusting' "; and, when Damon's speech about fundamental civil rights calls forth boos from the audience, she stands, shouts, and is forcibly removed from the room. But she is undismayed: she is sure that Edward would have been proud of Damon. As Fosca, who is now dead, had once asserted, the essence of Edward Cavan has remained to fortify his friends in their need.

Miss Sarton has said of *Faithful Are the Wounds* that it began as a question in her mind—Can a man be right and wrong at the same time?—and that therefore she could not make the book "move toward a complete justification of the main character." [2] She was more interested in the effect of his suicide on his friends and colleagues than in why he killed himself. Yet the fact that his associates cannot understand his reason for suicide enlarges Cavan's significance. He is seen as more than just a valuable member of society, the dissenter who is, in Damon's words, one of the "guardians of conscience" (133). He may have been wrong in his inflexibility, but in his fervor and love of humanity he is impressively right. The novel is, in fact, a plea like that of Francis Chabrier in *Shadow of a Man,* for people to become "more human." Tortured and despairing though Cavan is, he achieves human stature because of his intense caring about the welfare of all people.

Seen against the background of Cavan's suicide, the lives of most of the other characters seem too small, hedged in by doubts and self-seeking. As one reviewer said of the novel: "It is about modern affections, loyalties, sympathies, sentiments, the simple, ancient human attributes which, maimed, safeguarded and hoarded, leave only Self-Protection, alone and counting losses. Only the act of Self-Sacrifice remains; and from that base is all the new beginning. . . ." [3] Seen as self-sacrifice to which he was driven by people's blindness to the world's need, Cavan's act is inevitable for a man of his character. As a child, he was impressed by the contrast between the comfort of his own home and the barren conditions in homes of the door. Whether it was his mother's poetic temperament that gave him his intensity or his father's opposition that hardened him in his beliefs, he was enraged at injustice, hated thoughtless conformity, and never "played safe."

Isabel recalls how Cavan the boy used to get into fights and come home " 'with blood all over his mouth and that funny little look he had, as if he felt somehow—somehow—as if he'd crashed through' " (11). She also shows how such childhood incidents foreshadowed his death and answered the question of its "rightness": " 'I don't know how to say it, as if coming in to the house which was always so quiet, all bloody and dirty, he had won even when he had really lost' " (11). After his death, Cavan has "won" in that he has impressed indelibly on the minds of his friends and colleagues the need to be a "whole" person—involved in all of life with his entire being. Ivan Goldberg, who hated Cavan's being a kind of accusing conscience to him, sees after his death that Cavan's attempt was " 'to break through . . . a human barrier, to unite the intellect and life'" (192). And George Hastings, who had been only puzzled by Cavan's distress over persecution of the intellectuals, realizes that his greatness as a teacher came from his being as much involved in human affairs as in literature.

Cavan's tragedy, as his friend Orlando Fosca explains it, is that, despite his insight and his sympathy, he could not communicate "the very essence of his belief" (209). Isabel wishes that just once Edward had explained to her, without anger, the things most important to him; but Fosca explains that he could not, for "'When he fought you, he was fighting himself'" (209). Edward's loneliness is apparent, but what he most longed for was communion—the first and basic irony of the novel. He was separated from people partly by his very intensity; and this situation is what George finally understands, for Edward's passion was in one way similar to his for Pen. And the reader recalls a similar situation between characters in the earlier novels—Mark's passion for Georgia keeps him from knowing her: and Sally's for Violet keeps them from easy and relaxed talk. Though the passion in these instances is more personal than Edward's, the author is saying that any kind of too-great intensity shuts off communication.

Most of the main characters change and grow in the course of the novel. Damon Phillips, who impresses Isabel as being like a caricature of a professor—"his thin uncombed hair falling down over his forehead, his face all broken up by lines, his air of agitated incompetence" (170)—is, despite his intellectual brilliance, constantly fighting self-doubt. Yet in the last scene, where he appears before the committee investigating so-called Communist activities at Harvard, he shows remarkable poise and firmness. Time and thought and the memory of Edward's sacrifice have matured him. He says that "in the essence of his belief" Edward had been right. At the climax of his speech, Damon speaks of Edward's fear of "'the increasing apathy and retreat of the American people before such encroachments of fundamental civil rights as are represented by this committee'" (279). Not only is Edward's apparent radicalism justified here, but Damon gains in stature.

The change in Ivan Goldberg is even more noteworthy. Outwardly cold and collected, he suffers more than anyone would suspect; as a Jew, he feels he must surmount his feeling of defensiveness by being always in command of a situation; his

habitual shield is a little half-smile that makes him look supe-
rior and not quite human. After Edward's death, his self-doubt
at first becomes a self-hatred. He feels bitterly that he had failed
a man whom he greatly respected, and in the privacy of his own
home he weeps. Later, in a long talk with Isabel, he shows that
he knows his need to become more involved in the suffering of
other people. He sees the contrast between Edward's deep and
generous concern for the world and his own narrow absorption
in his academic subject. Though he still disagrees with Edward's
ideas about socialism, he says, " 'Who are we, unwilling or unable
to commit ourselves, to judge?' " (198). Edward had made him
expect more of himself—has, in a sense, forced him to grow. Yet
Isabel is not really at ease with Goldberg. His own pain seems to
make him wish to inflict pain—or perhaps he only wishes to en-
lighten her as he himself has become enlightened. But he is not
a pleasant person, as the following passages in their conversation
show:

> "I didn't know I was divided," Isabel said quickly. "I'm not."
> "Because, I suspect, you have like me deliberately chosen to
> shut yourself away from the agonies of your times. . . ."
>
> "And we're both wrong?" she asked. Goldberg pushed the
> cigarette out hard in the ash tray. "Not wrong, less than we might
> be, less than Edward was. But we'll live, Mrs. Ferrier, won't
> we?" He smiled his intolerable smile. (193–94)
>
> "Must one be 'committed' as you call it? Why can't people go
> about their business in peace?" she asked passionately. Every
> time she came close to people's feeling about Edward, Isabel felt
> as if she were being sucked down into a whirlpool where nothing
> was clear, where everything was struggle and agony.
> "There is a price to be paid for not participating and for re-
> fusing to be responsible. I wonder," Goldberg said, and she felt
> the slight barb in the question, "what price you have paid." (198)

This man who, in an agony of nervousness, meets Edward's seminar after the suicide, finds that he can make no reference to
him: "It was clear to him that if he even spoke Edward's name, his
voice would break, he would disgrace himself and be unable to
go on" (156). In the figure of Ivan Goldberg, Miss Sarton has
drawn one of her most perceptive and fascinating portraits.

Like Goldberg, George Hastings comes to see that Cavan's death has given him a responsibility—"to get through . . . to arrive at communion with other people somehow and at communion with a whole self in himself" (260). But the change in him is less striking—for he is young and ardent—than that in Isabel Ferrier. Miss Sarton has said that she began writing the novel with the idea that Isabel was to be treated ironically: "She was to incarnate the American middle-class woman, terrified of her radical brother (because he was so disturbing), clinging to the *status quo,* encased in a smug sense of superiority toward those conflicts which ended in suicide." [4] But Isabel refused to be an antiheroine. In order to understand the "forces which, at the time of McCarthy, seemed to be about to tear this country apart," [5] the author had to get inside Isabel; the result is that she is presented with sympathy.

Isabel's bewilderment and sense of alienation from her brother, her fears on entering the strange academic world of Cambridge, and above all her self-examination as she sits in Edward's empty apartment—these endear her to the reader and make her very real. In the apartment, thinking of their childhood, she sees that the incompatible marriage of their parents had made her long for a life of peace without tension; but, for Edward, it had had another effect: "It had made his loyalty intransigient and narrow, deepened him, tightened him, matured him—and, in the end, murdered him" (246). Although Isabel tries to dismiss her new insights as mere "emotional response," her realization of what it had been like for Edward to stand by and watch suffering is a crucial experience for her: "To be a witness, what could suggest more terrible responsibility? To have no human responsibilities such as marriage and children had been to her, but to be left, naked, the witness always, the one who is aware and can do nothing?" (246). From her conversations with Edward Cavan's colleagues, and now from looking about his rooms, she understands for the first time the pain of human existence—"the whole world like a cry, like a need—" (247), and it is difficult to believe that she will return unchanged to her secure life with Henry.

So it develops that, reacting to Cavan's death, some of the characters change: they grow in understanding and sympathy. In this second splendid irony of the novel, greater life comes from death. The ones who do not noticeably change—Julia,

Orlando Fosca, and Grace Kimlock—are already more open to the needs of others, less self-centered than the ones who are driven by Edward's action to a painful kind of stocktaking. Yet Julia, who had longed for Edward to be able to receive love or give it, feels a shocked guilt at her own complex reaction to the suicide. Though she does not feel so personally guilty as Damon does, she has a moment of relief, knowing that Edward's presence, like "some aching conscience," will not again trouble her and Damon. "At least now there would be no more arguments. There might be a little peace" (144). The author's revelation of the inevitable self-interest that intrudes on even the purest grief is in the tradition of the great Russian Realists like Tolstoy. A similar concern for self is George's swift recollection that Cavan would have got him an instructorship; he hates himself for thinking of it.

Grace Kimlock is an old woman, one who has been fighting the battles of the liberals for years, working for the persecuted and the underprivileged. Of all the characters, only she comes near to being a stereotype—the strong-minded, rather waspish New England spinster. She reacts to the news of Edward's death with grief that masquerades as anger; tells Orlando that she *must* know why Cavan did it, or she will die; and only after he has talked with her for a while does she confess how unbearably lonely she feels with Edward gone.

Orlando, like Grace, feels no guilt, nor does he know the wrenching of her loneliness; for he is—surprisingly in one so unassuming—nearly the "whole man." A fine scholar and teacher, caring about people, loving and yet detached, he grieves for Edward; but he would not have had him different from what he was. He thinks, "One cannot wish the people one loves to be other than they are. An Edward not torn to pieces, an Edward concerned only with literature, would seem a monster" (166). Sitting alone for the first time in many hours—for he had been the one summoned when the terrible news came—Orlando groans, not for himself so much as for the loss that Edward is to the university. He thinks of a chestnut tree he has recently seen that lost a branch in a storm, and the image haunts him in its suggestion of Edward's death: "This was the great tree standing with a limb torn off, bleeding into the air, that branch rich with leaves and flowers which would never grow back again, never bear its real fruit, that branch which had just fallen with a great crash" (165).

When Orlando first sees Grace after Cavan's death, he goes straight to where she is standing by her fireplace and embraces her; but the comforting gesture is refused. "She disengaged herself stiffly, turned her back on him, and said rather gruffly, as if the episode had not taken place, 'Where's Ellen with our tea?'" (158–59). She cannot admit to emotion yet, and Orlando reflects that she is always pushing life away from her or trying to hide from it. Here is a theme that is to become increasingly important in Miss Sarton's novels—the fear of feeling. Early in *Faithful Are the Wounds,* Isabel reflects that families are cruel because so often parents and children are afraid of showing their real affection for one another. Part of Edward's rebellion against his father may have come from Mr. Cavan's stiff withdrawal from any indication of his love for his son. And Isabel had loved her brother but could never let him know: "All through her childhood she had looked and looked at Edward, as if through a pane of glass, but she could never hug him. It was never simple" (14). George Hastings, too, thinks of how Edward had mutely asked his help in some problem: "I suppose, George thought, he wanted something of me that he couldn't ask, that I had to give. But I didn't give it. It was too big; it upset my feelings about things. It broke down walls like breaking down houses. . . . We're all so scared of our feelings . . ." (140). The fact that Cavan has "naked feeling" sets him apart and makes him the hero in a world where more and more people, the author implies, are turning away, like Grace, from spontaneous, openhearted emotion.

In addition to introducing new themes and subjects, the book also make more noticeable use of images to convey meaning than did Miss Sarton's previous novels. Fosca's thought of how the great tree, "wounded," reflects the university maimed by Edward's death, is echoed elsewhere in references to Edward himself as a wounded man. The guilty like to think of him as "sick" —as verging on insanity, but they are only trying to escape the attack made by his death on their own cloistered virtue. The reader is left feeling that a hard, self-seeking society has wounded him; but the depth of his love, which makes of him almost a Christ figure, causes Cavan to injure himself for the world's good. Such is the implication of the verse in Proverbs from which the book takes its title: "Faithful are the wounds of a friend."

The most frequent image is that of walls—used to show the divisions between people or the barriers that prevent the active, "human" participation in all life. Ivan Goldberg feels that mutual respect has brought Edward and him so close to being friends that only "a thin glass [exists] between them" (108), but he cannot slide it away with goodwill alone; since he thinks of Edward's concern for academic freedom as only a "morbid sense of responsibility," the door between them, literally and metaphorically, closes. Similarly, Isabel remembers how their father and Edward had "walled themselves in against each other" (202); and she herself, when she finds that she can talk freely to Damon and Julia about her brother, becomes almost afraid. "She felt as if a high wall had just fallen down, the wall that had protected her, and now she was naked. She had given herself away. 'I must go,' she said, getting up as if actually to run away." (208).

As someone who has chosen the opposite way of life from Edward's, Isabel is frequently spoken of in association with walls. At her luncheon with Goldberg, at a French restaurant where, he says, they will feel "less exposed" than at the Faculty Club, Goldberg tells her she has, like him, remained safely outside of the agonies of their time. They have, he means, erected walls. The idea returns to her forcibly when she faces herself and her life in Edward's apartment. Here she seems to be asking questions of the very walls, which, like her dead brother, do not answer. But she admits honestly that she and her husband, in their luxurious house with its swimming pool and deep freeze, its bridge games and cocktails, have paid a price for remaining "secure behind the walls of their life" (247). They have been less than fully human.

Similar to the image of walls is that of prisons. Julia, another person who desperately questions the silent walls of her house after Edward's death, feels at times imprisoned in her "narrow resentment of Damon" (229). Edward is not the only one who feels in a prison and is tapping on the walls, as Orlando imagines, in a frantic attempt to communicate. The prison image, like that of walls, indicates the loneliness of each human being who, caught in his own personality and inheritance, longs at times for real communion with others. The theme of human loneliness, developed in *Shower of Summer Days*, returns in this novel in a more tragic context.

In some of her poetry, particularly in *The Lion and the Rose* and in *The Land of Silence,* Miss Sarton has expressed the idea that everyone should show active concern for the suffering of all people in all places; but most of her poems on this theme are too obvious and lack the grace and music of her best verses. Her fictional treatment of this appeal "to the living" is much more effective. *Faithful Are the Wounds* transcends in its meaning the particular era of American history in which it is set. Instead, it has a universal theme—the urgent need for man to be his brother's keeper.

II *The Birth of a Grandfather* (1957)

In her next novel, *The Birth of a Grandfather,* Miss Sarton again uses the New England setting—the Wyeth family live in Cambridge; and, like the Bradfords and others in *Shadow of a Man,* they spend their summers on the Maine coast. A novel about family relationships and the difficulty of communication between husband and wife, parents and children, its themes have been touched upon in earlier books but are more fully developed here. The title refers to Sprig Wyeth, who, with his wife Frances is in early middle age. Their daughter Betsy, who marries Tom Dorgan, has a child, whose impending arrival marks for Sprig the beginning of a new phase in his life.

The three divisions of the novel indicate the pain of the spiritual rebirth that must be undergone, not only by Sprig, but also to some extent by Frances. Part I, "The Island," tells of a family vacation on the island in Maine; but it bears the obvious symbolism of the isolation of each individual, their reaching out to one another across inevitable divisions. Part II, "Children of the Ice Age," shows the emotional tightness and inability to give of self which maintains tension within the family; and in Part III, "The Birth of a Grandfather," there is an indication that Sprig has found a more mature philosophy that will keep his marriage on a steadier plane as he and Frances approach old age.

The idea that only in old age do people attain real maturity and know themselves is suggested in the first part in the character of Aunt Jane, ninety and very frail, who has a strong spiritual influence on all the others. She and Sprig's father, called Gran-Quan, live together and have come to the island as usual to be part of the Wyeth summer. Others who are there are Caleb, the son of the family, a senior at Harvard; Sprig's unmarried sister, a teacher; Betsy and her fiancé, Tom Dorgan; and, for short periods, Uncle Joe and Frances' good friend Lucy, whose husband has left her.

The center and heart of the family is Frances, whose energy and passion remind the reader of Melanie in *The Bridge of Years*. On the first morning of the story, Francis finds Sprig in the wood where he has been chopping trees, and as they sit on the grass watching Caleb sail, she knows that Sprig does not want "to be reminded of that hour of passion in the night" (12); he has retreated into his habitual reserve. Frances feels there is always a tenseness between them. An even greater tension exists between Sprig and Caleb, who wants to be treated as an individual on his own, not just as the son of the family. Yet, for all the difficulties among them, there is a solidarity about the Wyeth clan that makes Tom Dorgan feel them to be a powerful entity, bound together by all they have shared.

On July Fourth, the whole family sails to a more distant island for its annual picnic supper. Tom and Lucy have returned to the city, but they are joined by Uncle Joe and by Sprig's friend Bill Waterford. Aunt Jane feels strangely dizzy and weak but does not complain when even the slight exertion of getting out of the boat seems almost impossibly difficult. During the display of fireworks that ends the evening, Jane dies so quietly that at first only her brother Joe, sitting near her, is sure that she has gone. Caleb and Betsy sail back alone in his boat, wondering how the death will affect their parents, who seem to the children strangely innocent and vulnerable.

In Part II, Gran-Quan, who is in a nursing home, is trying to die, for his existence seems meaningless after Jane's death. Life in the house at Cambridge continues in its usual pattern, with Caleb more than ever rebellious. When Betsy comes to the house one afternoon to say that she is to have a baby, Sprig is pleased that Betsy intends to name the child, if it is a boy, after his grandfather; but he is also oddly troubled by Betsy's news. He feels that his own marriage has never been happy, that he is constantly failing Frances; and the idea of perpetuating the family, with its tangle of emotional demands, upsets him.

While he, Frances, and Hester are still at dinner, Sprig receives a telephone call from his old friend Thorny Stiles, who reports that Bill Waterford has lung cancer and will probably live only six months. Sprig goes to see Thorny, and shortly afterward Bill unexpectedly arrives to ask Thorny not to reveal the truth to his wife, Nora; for her day-to-day life, if she knows, will be intolerable. Sprig returns home reluctantly, feeling that life has become unbearable; he longs more than ever to escape from all his responsibilities as a husband and a father. Bill, with his gaiety, his enormous zest for life, has sustained Sprig in a way that he is only beginning to understand.

The father-son antagonism reaches its climax one Sunday when Tom, Betsy, and Hester have come to dinner, and Sprig and Caleb quarrel over the boy's wish to spend a year abroad. Caleb leaves the table in anger and goes to his room; Betsy follows to try to comfort him; but she returns to tell her father that, in his anxiety not to spoil Caleb, he is ruining his life. Hester and Frances try to show him that, if he sends the boy abroad, he will not be "rewarding indolence" (155) but helping Caleb find out, completely on his own, what he wants to be. Sprig admits he has been wrong, goes to his son, and they are reconciled. Sprig offers to give him the money for Europe if he will wait until after their usual summer in Maine. It is as if Bill Waterford's illness and the knowledge that he soon will die make Sprig gradually more understanding of other people and less shy about speaking of his own feelings.

After Sprig has made peace with Caleb, he asks Frances to go for a walk, realizing how he has failed her in recent years. When he goes to see Bill (and finds to his surprise that he likes Nora, whom he has never really known or wanted to know), Sprig reveals, in answer to their questions, that the two things he most cares about in the world are formal gardens and translating Greek plays; he also comes close to forming a definite idea as to what he thinks is the purpose of life, concluding that it has to do, not with outer achievement, but with building character. Yet he cannot tell Frances this, and the tension between them remains.

When Part III opens, their marriage seems in an even more precarious state than before. Sprig is now wholly absorbed in Bill's dying, and Frances gets none of his attention; for, when he is not at Bill's house, he is secluded in the barn, playing Haydn masses. The summer on the island is this time dealt with in only one chapter, showing Frances in a state of muted sadness that is almost apathy. Yet, when they return to Cambridge, she recovers her spirits in the golden autumn days, and, after a visit with Lucy one afternoon, she decides to stop to see Bill. Even though he must gasp for breath, Bill tells her of his concern about what will happen to Sprig after his death. Sprig, he says, "must begin it"—meaning a less self-absorbed life.

On a night in early October, Nora calls to ask Sprig to come. She says that Bill wants to die; and Sprig, telling her that she must let Bill go, suddenly realizes that what he had thought was his love for his friend has really been self-love in disguise. Frances, left at home in desolation, recognizes on the same evening that she must detach herself from dependence on Sprig—like Nora, she must "let him go." The next morning, when Thorny arrives to tell them Bill has died, both Frances and Sprig feel, after the shock of grief, that there is a new understanding between them: she has "learned to withhold," and Sprig has "within the limits of his temperament, learned to give . . ." (270). When Betsy's boy is born, Sprig has another revelation of what life can be; for he finds it is more important to think of the child than of himself. He also realizes that what he and Frances are together transcends their individual entities. He is at last learning something about love.

The Birth of a Grandfather, coming only two years after *Faithful Are the Wounds,* shows the author's continuing concern with the loneliness of people—their need for communion, which at the same time must leave them free as unique individuals. In this later novel, the scope is more limited; whereas Edward Cavan's lack of communion symbolizes man alone in the universe, Sprig Wyeth's plight arises from the New England temperament and stands at the center of tensions within his family. Sprig fears that, if he gives more of himself to other people, he will somehow lose his identity. Throughout the novel, he is unable to make "any final and absolute gift of the self." He fears that if one does, "then you were no longer safe, separate, you were caught. You might be destroyed" (30). So burdensome does the guilt about his own withdrawal become that he wishes constantly to escape, to leave his family to return to Japan, where he had visited as a young man. After he knows of Bill's illness, he feels more than ever "empty." Thinking of his children and of Bill and Thorny, he reflects: "They know what they're doing . . . and I'm walking in the dark, a kind of monster who has neither been a real husband nor a real father, nor perhaps even a real friend" (134).

Such is the state of individualism or egotism pushed to its limit. Sprig's failure to achieve communion comes—not from too much love as Cavan's does—but from a complete lack of understanding of selfless love, which he begins to approach only after Bill's death. Yet Sprig is drawn as a character with whom the reader sympathizes, for his very awareness of his coldness and imprisonment within the self makes him touchingly alive.

Sprig's greatest failure in communion is within his marriage. Though he and Frances have been "happily" married for twenty years, she feels that they are at a distance from each other. Even in physical intercourse they remain separate: "Their union was not the flowing together of two deeply joined selves, but only a desperate moment of possession of each other, which disappointed because something was always withheld" (5). Frances has long seen the difference between her marriage and that of her mother and father; she recalls the "immense warmth" there, how they "walked down the garden together in the evening, the way life flowed between them, unstopped, unstinted . . ." (14). And, as she sees something of the same love between Betsy and Tom, she envies her daughter a deeper communion in marriage than she herself has ever known.

Frances, like Sprig, is a completely believable character. At times she seems too demanding, constantly wanting more affection than her undemonstrative husband can show, giving way to tears so much that she seems a quivering mass of sensibility. But again, with the inconsistency of real people, she shows her fortitude, her enormous patience at the times when she appears to herself to be nothing but a cook, caterer, and general servant in Sprig's house. The reader sees her appearing always "airy and bright" (135) with Sprig to try to hide her own hurt and sense of loss. And Sprig understands something of her feelings; in a moment of insight, he sees how he has made her shy in his presence by the barrier he has erected. "The realization of how he had abandoned her right there within the walls of the house, and of their life, suddenly broke over him." Yet he cannot ease the situation, for "the awful thing was that knowing something did

not make one able to do anything about it. The more he saw, the
more he felt incapable . . ." (168).

Both of them think, now and then, of divorce. A teasing
thought, it cannot be fully suppressed, as they drift farther and
farther apart during Bill's illness. It is as if both are dying—Bill
and the Wyeth marriage. Bill, who had seemed so enormously
vital, like a great tree firmly planted in the midst of life, can die.
And if so, can anything that seems durable, like a marriage, really
survive?

Most of the Wyeths' problems seem, in the end, to be focused
on the painful transition they are making in middle age. The time
of youth, when everything seemed possible and somehow endur-
ing, is past. Both Sprig and Frances wonder if there will be time
for them to become themselves, a personality apart from family
ties. Sprig's longing to go to Japan and Frances' momentary rebellion against sewing on her husband's buttons—these are symp-
toms of their feeling that time is slipping away before they
have attained the spiritual stature that in youth seemed always
just ahead. After Betsy has told them she is to have a child, and
Sprig, Frances, and Hester are alone for dinner, Frances proposes
a toast, not to the child but, as she says, " 'to us . . . not to our
family selves, not to this web of relationships, but to our secret
selves, whoever they may be' " (117). And when Frances talks
with Lucy about her divorce, she tells her that " 'You'll have a
chance to find out who you are' " (44).

Yet Frances, though she wants to keep her identity, believes
that personality can be developed through and with others and
not in withdrawal into some secret place where nobody can follow. In this respect, she differs from her husband who believes
that, in the midst of all the drastic changes that life brings, one
must hold onto some permanent core of the self that is detached
from all other people. He has not learned, as Paul Duchesne in
Bridge of Years finally did, that there can be "positive detachment."

Sprig, afraid of being absorbed by other people, only gradually
sees that the self becomes whole and integrated by giving—that
he must lose his life to save it. His friend Thorny Stiles tells him
that his grief and bewilderment over Bill's approaching death
and Frances' unhappiness cannot be lightened by his withdrawal:
he must "let in" what he fears; he must become more involved.

Thorny's words, repeated for emphasis, are "'not by withholding . . .'" (214).

The need for a spiritual rebirth, which runs through this novel,
is paralleled in Miss Sarton's poetry of about the same date—
particularly in the volume entitled *In Time Like Air*. In the novel,
the theme comes through not only in Sprig's struggle but also in
images of enclosure that emphasize personal withholding and the
restricting nature of family life. As the baby in Betsy's womb
comes forth in due time, so Sprig breaks out of his personality.
The family as an institution is seen as both good and bad. It is
good because it provides continuity and a place where psychic
wounds can heal. Aunt Jane's reflections voice the author's
thoughts, not only in this novel, but in others such as *The Bridge
of Years:* "The family was what consoled, sheltered, kept the past
and present flowing together; understood things without being
told, remembered names when you forgot them" (42).

But it is bad that the family can restrict, as is shown in Caleb's
experience. He feels bound to his parents in a painful way, as if
they represent a debt that he can never pay. Even when he is
happily preparing to break away by going for a year to Greece,
he knows that he will take with him the memory of his parents'
present misery. In a last talk with Betsy, he says of Frances and
Sprig: "'They're so terribly controlled. They imprison each other.
. . . And this is supposed to be a happy marriage'" (248). The
image of the prison, or someone locked up, is used in this novel,
as in *Faithful Are the Wounds*, to show the need for greater communion and for freedom of the individual within the family
group.

Perhaps the best image of the family, showing its double nature as both shelter and prison, is given in the observation of Tom
Dorgan on his first visit to the island: "Now he and Betsy had
found a haven on the window seat where they could hold hands
unobserved. Tom looked out into the great cavelike room, fire-
light throwing shadows on the ceiling, and everything here massive and dark. The Aladdin lamp made a circle of bright light
around the old man sitting in an armchair, a book open on his
knees" (15). It is a memorable and ambivalent picture. Soon all
the Wyeths will assemble to listen to Gran-Quan, a patriarchal
figure, read Wordsworth's poetry aloud. So it has always been during summer on the island. Patterns are so fixed that, when Caleb

wants to break them, he feels both anger and guilt. It is not only the room in this picture that is in partial darkness; the family relationship conceals hidden angers and resentments. Yet the bright light on the book perhaps shows the Wyeths' traditional reliance on intellect or on the truth of poetry that can free them from forces "massive and dark."

Miss Sarton herself evinces in this novel the same ability that a reviewer of *Faithful Are the Wounds* found remarkable—the ability to "turn to light what is shadowed, raise to the level of common ground what is half-buried underground." [6] One thinks of how often someone with cancer is spoken of in hushed tones, almost as if he were already dead. In *The Birth of a Grandfather,* the relationship between the ill person and his friends and relatives is treated with candor. Bill asks his doctor not to reveal the truth to his wife until he has been able to achieve some detachment. The suffering of his wife and Sprig is revealed, as is their necessary acceptance, at last, of the fact that Bill wants to die. And just as the author considers such subjects in the novel, the characters also feel a sense of relief when hitherto unbroached subjects are openly examined.

What, finally, is the significance of the novel in the sequence of Miss Sarton's work? It must be admitted that it breaks no new ground; for even the theme of rebirth, made specific here, was approached in the previous treatment of other middle-aged characters such as Isabel Ferrier in *Faithful Are the Wounds* and Violet Gordon in *A Shower of Summer Days.* The author again presents her faith in man's intellect and in his need for continuity with the past. The New England scene, faithfully portrayed, has also been beautifully presented before. But this comparison does not imply that *The Birth of a Grandfather* is valueless. It does, however, rework familiar material, and the themes are stressed rather too much. The conflict between generations, for example, is too heavily underlined. The novel lacks the brilliance of technique of *Shower of Summer Days,* which leaves more to the reader's imagination; and it lacks the tragic implications of *Faithful Are the Wounds.* Although consistently interesting, it is not a memorable achievement.

III *The Small Room* (1961)

In her next novel, *The Small Room,* Miss Sarton explored relationships and communication on a college campus. Although the academic world had been the background of Edward Cavan's tragedy in *Faithful Are the Wounds,* this later novel presents a quite different picture. It is not a large university but a women's college in New England; and, though some of the types of academic person are similar in the two novels, most of the teachers in *The Small Room* are women who are absorbed in their work in a way that is more personal, more intense, than that of most men teachers.

The story is told throughout from the point of view of Lucy Winter, a young teacher who has just received her doctor's degree and is on her way, when the book opens, to Appleton College for her first job. She has broken her engagement to John; and, throughout the novel, her painful remembrance of that unhappy love affair runs as a kind of minor theme. Lucy finds her colleagues and students extremely interesting. At a tea given by Hallie Summerson, the head of the English Department, she meets Henry Atwood and his wife Deborah, who are also new at the college; Jack Beveridge, who teaches Romance languages, and his wife Maria; Jennifer Finch of the Mathematics Department; and the famous Carryl Cope, who teaches medieval history and inspires everyone with awe. Lucy learns that Appleton College has a reputation for fostering the brilliant student, and she approaches her first class with some trepidation.

After her lecture, she is embarrassed by Pippa Brentwood, a student who wants to confide something about her father's death. Lucy feels that a teacher's relationship to students should be kept on a professional basis; but, on another day when she sees Pippa in a conference and learns the whole story, she feels pity for the girl and speaks to her gently. Afterward she reflects that knowledge cannot be taught in a vacuum; feelings are also important. This theme is dominant in the novel—that one must teach the "whole person"; the mind cannot be trained on its own. At a dinner given by the Beveridges, Lucy hears additional discussion about getting a resident psychiatrist for Appleton; she learns that Olive Hunt, a member of the board of directors and a good friend of Carryl Cope's, is strongly opposed to such an appointment, feeling that students should handle their own problems.

At the first faculty meeting, the possible dismissal of a student is discussed—she is Agnes Skeffington, a girl who has become so absorbed in working out an unusual mathematical problem that she now attends no classes or meetings and refuses to do any other work until the problem is finished. Her professor says that she is a near genius and should be allowed to continue at Appleton; others object that she will become too specialized and not receive a liberal education. Carryl Cope makes a strong plea that Agnes be kept, feeling that objectors are unwilling to "pay the price of excellence." The vote is close, but Agnes is allowed to stay. After the meeting, Lucy goes home with Carryl for a drink and learns more about the life of this unusual teacher and scholar. She also meets Olive Hunt. Before Lucy leaves, Carryl asks her to read an essay by her most brilliant student, Jane Seaman, which has been published in a college magazine.

Most of the plot revolves around Jane Seaman, the bright senior from a broken home who, Lucy discovers, is guilty of plagiarism. As she reads the essay on the *Iliad,* Lucy realizes that she has seen it before, and next day at the library she traces it to Simone Weil's little-known essay published in a British magazine. After consulting Hallie Summerson, Lucy calls in Jane for a talk before the news is broken to Carryl Cope. Jane tells, after trying at first to deny the charge, of how the pressure on her to produce excellent papers had become so great she could no longer endure it: "'The more you do, the more you're expected to do, and each thing has got to be better, always better'" (100). Lucy feels that subconsciously the girl had wanted to have the plagiarism discovered, so that the pressure on her would cease; someone—probably Carryl Cope—has failed with Jane.

Lucy is now more than ever convinced that "teaching is first of all teaching a person" (104). Later she is surprised to find that Carryl takes the blame on herself, realizing that she has pushed Jane too hard. Jane's theft is, she sees, an attack on *her,* and she is grieved by what she has done to a student. But, in trying mercifully to keep the matter quiet, she has reckoned without the other students. Rumors about the plagiarism are soon all over the campus, and Pippa comes to tell Lucy that Jane is thought to be unfairly sheltered from the consequences of her action; therefore, she is being ostracized by other students.

Tension among the faculty also arises. Maria Beveridge, who is not an intellectual and who resents her husband's admiration of Carryl, says at a party given by the Atwoods that Carryl feels guilty and is "protecting an investment" (144) by trying to keep the plagiarism quiet. In spite of Jennifer's attempts to calm them, Jack and Maria become furious with each other, and the party ends in embarrassment and bad feeling. That same evening, Jane knocks on Lucy's door at the Faculty Club and comes in drunk. Lucy makes coffee, and during their talk she learns how lost the girl feels and how deeply she hates Carryl. She invites Jane to come home with her for Thanksgiving vacation and see a psychiatrist.

On their return to the campus, President Blake Tillotson calls a meeting of several faculty with the dean, Miss Valentine, to discuss the crisis. Students are now demanding that Jane be tried by the usual process of their government; and, because of angry comments flying about among them as well as among the faculty, the matter must now be dealt with openly. Lucy goes to the meeting wondering if she will be blamed for having taken Jane to see a psychiatrist. Jack Beveridge tells her privately that the tension with Maria has increased and that their marriage is almost wrecked. Others at the meeting with Jack are Hallie Summerson and Jennifer Finch; President Tillotson has not asked Carryl because she is too personally involved in the affair. Hostility on the campus is directed not only at Jane, who has escaped punishment, but also at Carryl, who had had power enough to shield the student. After a long, difficult discussion, the group decides to put the case to the whole faculty in the light that Lucy sees it—that Jane has been a victim of the overemphasis on intellectual achievement at Appleton, and that a resident psychiatrist is desirable. Jane has, they realize, projected her conflict onto Carryl, but it stems partly from her unhappy home situation; and, had a psychiatrist been present, the crisis might not have happened. Tillotson regretfully gives up hope of Olive Hunt's millions, as she has said she will not leave money to the college if the psychiatrist is engaged.

At the faculty meeting, "a battering, shattering experience" (183), Carryl says that she had been wrong and now wants Jane

judged by the faculty and students in the usual way. But she confesses to Lucy later, when they are having a cocktail, that her
prestige among both faculty and students is now very low. She is
also depressed because Olive Hunt will be furious about the decision to appoint a psychiatrist. As they talk, Olive arrives, and an
argument begins over her now not wanting to leave her money
to Appleton. Carryl says that, although Olive has the right to
leave her money where she will, using it "to browbeat people" is
a misuse, just as she, Carryl, had "misused power to try to cover
for Jane" (191). She also asserts that, if Olive removes herself
from Appleton, she will at the same time end their friendship.
The quarrel comes to no conclusion, for Tillotson telephones to
say that the student council has acquitted Jane and asked that the
college receive her back since she has already been punished
enough "through the long delay and suspension of justice" (198).

At a pre-Christmas party at Hallie's, Carryl insists on discussing the Seaman affair and on understanding how her colleagues
feel about her part in it. She acknowledges that, when Jane came
and went freely in her house, it was not because she wanted
books or intellectual exchange but because she had somehow
wanted help that Carryl had not given. What, she asks them, had
she withheld from Jane? In the end, Jennifer realizes that what
Carryl had withheld was love; and Carryl admits she had been
afraid to show it. The novel ends with Carryl's inviting Lucy for
supper after the party, admitting that she is lonely without Olive,
and talking about her own life and Lucy's future. Lucy feels that,
when she has overcome the hurt of her broken engagement, she
might, inspired by Carryl and the others at Appleton, become
completely committed to teaching.

The Small Room is a perceptive and sympathetic portrayal of
the inner life of the teacher. As in her previous novels, Miss Sarton brings to light truths that, though sensed by some people,
have seldom been dealt with in fiction. And she shows an awareness of the intricacies of campus politics and the possibility of
moral conflict in a college community. But, though the plot of
The Small Room has suspense and excitement, the core of the
novel is not the question of what will happen to Jane Seaman or
whether the pattern of Carryl Cope's personal relationships will

change. Rather, it is the author's intensely interesting analysis of the college teacher's job.

Lucy realizes, from visiting a class of Hallie Summerson's, that the great teacher induces learning as it cannot ever quite come about without his providing the living contact between the student and his books. Hallie's skill in leading a discussion of Keats' letters, her knowing how to direct and channel enthusiasm, and her giving a clear line to the questions and answers is like the skill of a composer in a fugue; and her masterly summation near the end of the hour has been made possible by all the talk that has gone before: "Never, Lucy felt sure, would Hallie Summerson be able to speak to one person as she now did to sixty. Something streamed out of her was was absolutely open, passionate . . . the freeing of a *daimon*. . . . It surrounded Hallie Summerson with the aura of a person set apart, lonely and—Lucy half-smiled at the word, but uttered it to herself nevertheless—sacred" (116).

Lucy sees the great teacher, who can be, like Hallie, "a plain middle-aged woman in shabby classroom" (115) as someone with "immense inner reserve" and a "dedicated life." If the skill, power, and dedication of the teacher gave the whole picture of the profession, it would be highly idealized. Miss Sarton also shows the teacher as in conflict with himself, doubting the value of his work, wondering about his methods with students. An image in the Prologue of the novel indicates this theme. As Lucy is riding in the train, going north from New York, "Suddenly, by some trick of light, she was confronted by her own face, standing out enormous against a white farm and rocky pasture . . ." (11). She wonders for a moment if she really knows herself, and her examination of her face in the train window stands as a symbol of the self-examination that is constantly going on among the teachers at Appleton. Hallie Summerson says, as Lucy is leaving after her first tea party, " 'Is there a life more riddled with self-doubt than that of a woman professor, I wonder?' " (29). And by the end of her first three months of teaching—the time span of the novel—Lucy finally understands the question.

The question of the price of excellence is a basic theme of the novel. Carryl Cope, in the faculty meeting where Agnes Skeffington is discussed, says forthrightly that her colleagues talk a great deal about excellence but are unwilling to pay the price, which is, she believes, " 'eccentricity, maladjustment if you will, isolation of one sort or another, strangeness, narrowness' " (69). After this meeting, Agnes' name is hardly mentioned again, but Carryl's words remain in the reader's mind when Jane Seaman, also a brilliant student, fails in a more serious way to conform to the rules. How much is Jane's maladjustment the result of Appleton's emphasis on high achievement? Is Carryl right in saying that the price of excellence is some kind of strangeness or isolation? Near the end of the novel, someone asks why the word in connection with excellence is always *price;* why, she wonders, can it not instead be *joy.* And Jennifer answers that it is because " 'we have —haven't we, Carryl?—come to equate excellence with some sort of mutilation' " (233).

Whether or not excellence always means the sacrifice of a more normal and joyous life is never really answered. The author throws it out to the reader to contemplate. But this question is also related to another that is central in the story—the extent to which a teacher should be involved in students' private lives. Lucy is disturbed by Pippa's appeals for sympathy after her father's death, and Carryl does not give Jane the love she needs, thus helping to drive her in desperation to plagiarism. Both the younger and the older teacher have an ingrained belief that their business is to train the mind; and, although they really know that mind and emotions cannot be separated, they want, as Lucy tells herself, "to teach . . . in peace . . . without all this personal stuff" (51). But it cannot be done in peace. She realizes quite soon that she cannot be exclusively concerned with knowledge, that "intellectual brilliance divorced from life" (128) cannot be defended. Thus, the novel presents questions that are crucial in the world of learning; and these questions are made dramatic by the painful situation of Jane Seaman, the student who is driven to dishonesty and suffers a near breakdown; by the dilemma facing the college over employing a psychiatrist for students and thereby losing Olive Hunt's millions, money sorely needed; and by the strange, conflicted mind of Carryl Cope, who towers over the book as she towers intellectually over her colleagues.

Carryl is similar to other passionate characters of Miss Sarton, but she is at the same time unique. An outstanding scholar of medieval history who could have gone to any of the famous universities, she has chosen to remain at Appleton because she feels that teaching women is "a special kind of challenge" (247). She says frankly that she teaches for the exceptional person, and she has no patience with ignorance and sloth. Though a small woman physically, she gives an impression of power; people sense a hardness in her, a rigid control of emotion. Her eyes, which can look hooded like a hawk's, and her habit of "pouncing" in a conversation make her formidable. Her vitality makes Lucy compare her also to a tiger, and Carryl herself says she is committed to teaching " 'because a fire burns in my head' " (249).

Carryl's strength of feeling has been directed not to people but to her work. In all other areas, she has distrusted her own emotion. Afraid of feeling, she has severely disciplined herself to appear unmoved by people; for this reason, she is unable to communicate to Jane the love that the girl sorely needs. An indication of Carryl's greatness is her acknowledgment of this truth when she finally sees it. She admits that she had refused to consider more than Jane's mind, yet she loved Jane. Olive tells Lucy of how much the girl meant to Carryl and of how much she has suffered, wondering how she could help the student in the crisis.

With Carryl it is, in fact, a failure in communication rather like the failure of Edward Cavan of *Faithful Are the Wounds*. Both of them lack the detachment necessary to communicate love; they care too much and have not achieved the detachment that made Persis Bradford in *Shadow of a Man* such a powerful influence on people. All of Miss Sarton's treatments of the subject make clear that true detachment is only possible to a passionate person. It is not feeling itself that should be condemned; Carryl fails, not because she loves, but because she fears her own emotion instead of accepting it. Her story shows, as does that of Sprig Wyeth, that denying or suppressing feeling only creates suffering. Detachment, however, brings peace and fulfillment. The achievement is what T. S. Eliot is talking about when he writes, "Teach us to care and not to care." [7]

Perhaps one reason for Carryl's lack of detachment is the very smallness of the academic world she inhabits. Along with her appreciation of the art of the teacher, Miss Sarton has an awareness of the tensions that rise to an extreme height within the closed circle of the campus. The word "small" is used not only of Lucy's office but also of Hallie's living room and other rooms where the professors meet for drinks and talk. It suggests the

confinement that might produce intellectual work but that could
also cause emotional chaos. Carryl, refuting the idea that a college is "a safe little world," says to Lucy, "'It's simply a microcosm where every normal instinct and emotion gets raised to the
nth power'" (122). The idea of enclosure as related to intensity
gives rise to many animal images throughout the novel. This college world is like a zoo, and both students and faculty are compared to creatures of the animal and bird kingdom. The students,
not so individualized as the faculty, are compared to flocks of
starlings, "perpetual chatter and perpetual motion" (30); or,
when Lucy is angry with their lethargy, she says to them, "'Wake
up! . . . It's nine o'clock in the morning and you look like a drove
of whales washes up by the tide'" (107). Her freshman section,
she often feels, is so lacking in animation that it is like a "huge
passive elephant she had to try to lift . . ." (45).

Images for the faculty are of more alarming creatures. Professor March, when he is presenting the case of Agnes Skeffington, likens them to formidable lions. Carryl glares like a tiger and
sometimes shows her claws; but, towards the end of the book,
when she is attacked by furious adverse opinion on the campus,
she is compared to a desperate fox with the hounds after her.
Both students and faculty, at this point, are called a "wolf pack
in full cry" (172); and Jane feels caught, like an animal, by all
the strong feelings that cage her in. Jennifer Finch, after trying
unsuccessfully to calm the heated quarrel at the Atwoods' party,
suggests "'Perhaps it is time we retired to our separate lairs'"
(152).

Such images, and many more like them, show both the vitality
and the anguish of the college world, refuting the idea of the
"quiet groves of academe." One of the most powerful of the
images is caused by Lucy's intense pity for Olive Hunt and
Carryl when their long friendship is broken by the quarrel over
a psychiatrist for Appleton. Olive, hating herself but unable to
change her stubborn resistance, seems near despair. And Lucy
thinks, "Everything's so ragged and unfinished. Does life really
go on tearing at people's vitals forever like some cruel bird of
prey? Is there never to be rest or peace, no final and abiding wisdom or fulfillment?" (208). This question, with its weight of
suffering, runs through the whole novel. It defines the tone as

much as does the strong conviction about the importance of the teacher that the book communicates.

IV *Three Short Novels*

Four years after the appearance of *The Small Room*, Miss Sarton published *Mrs. Stevens Hears the Mermaids Singing*, which has been discussed in connection with her theory of poetry. Before and after the publication of *Mrs. Stevens*, she wrote three shorter works of fiction, *Joanna and Ulysses* (1963); *Miss Pickthorn and Mr. Hare* (1966); and *The Poet and the Donkey* (1969). In all of these, the dramatic action is chiefly internal, in the manner already established in her full-length novels; but in the three shorter works both plot and characterization have become so simplified that the effect is almost that of allegory.

Joanna, the heroine of the first "tale," as the author calls it, is a young Greek woman who goes to spend a month on the tiny island of Santorini. In this long-delayed holiday, she hopes not only to paint but also to recover her "real self" which has become almost buried during the years when she and her father have been recovering from the effects of war. Her family had helped prisoners escape from the Germans; her mother had been killed and her brother made deaf by torture. Since then, Joanna has patiently cared for her father, doing office work that she dislikes, instead of painting, because she must help earn their living. Now, with a month of freedom ahead, she is exhilarated; and, when she arrives at the marketplace of Santorini and sees a donkey being mistreated, she at first tries to turn away from the sight of more pain and bondage. But she cannot; the animal's belly is covered with sores and he will soon die if not removed from his cruel owners. Recklessly, Joanna buys him and takes him with her as she goes to find a lodging place.

Her first night is spent in an abandoned chapel, but the next day she persuades a woman to rent her a room. Ulysses, as she has called the donkey, is not a welcome guest because he eats everyone's flowers; but she arranges to tie him in the chapel at night and during the day to take him out on the hillsides with her. Her first job, though, is to cure his wounds, which she gradually does with many tubes of salve from the druggist and some old burlap bags. Ulysses responds quickly to kindness. She begins to think that, in saving him, she has also somehow saved herself, for she now begins to paint more seriously than ever before. She spends long days working in the open air and feels a wonderful new happiness. Her only human companion is a small boy, Nicholas, who expresses to her the curiosity of others in the village—why is she alone? Why has she not married? She tells him about her family and finds a release from tension in at last talking of her mother and of the pain of the war years.

As the month draws to an end, Joanna sadly realizes she must also leave Ulysses, and she persuades a kindhearted donkey driver to accept him as a gift. But, as her boat is leaving the quay, Ulysses strains forward on his rope, wanting to follow; and, when he utters "a piercing bray" (88), Joanna realizes she cannot leave him behind. She returns and takes him with her two days later on the freighter. With the help of a friend in Piraeus, she brings Ulysses home to Athens and hides him in the cellar, afraid to tell her father that he is there. For now, more than ever, Ulysses seems to her a symbol of her new self—the free person, the painter, discovered on Santorini—and she dreads returning to her role of housekeeper, nurse, and office worker.

But the presence of Ulysses, which her father soon discovers, leads to better understanding between father and daughter. When his refusal to take the donkey seriously angers her, he cries out in protest, " 'Don't just stand there . . . looking like your mother!' " (123). As if his words break an evil spell, they can now communicate naturally again, for this is the first time in ten years that he has spoken of his wife. At last they both understand that the past should not be buried but lived with. Her father sees, on looking at her paintings, that she has real talent; and he insists that she give up her office job and try to become a painter. Happy in her new life, she is willing to let Ulysses go to a friend of hers on the island of Mykonos.

There are, from the first, religious associations with Ulysses. His patience under his suffering and his quiet, meditative air suggest that he is a symbol of Joanna's soul. Just as the great sores on his belly have not been able to heal until she rescues him, so do her own psychic wounds from the war remain raw. Her first step toward recovering or developing her real self comes when she looks steadfastly at suffering—both Ulysses' and her own. Together they spend their first night in a chapel—suggestive of the spiritual nature of Joanna's quest. Her inability to part with the donkey as she is leaving Santorini (she has not yet achieved her soul's freedom) is emphasized by the high wind and rough sea as she sets out the first time. In contrast, her second departure, with Ulysses, is on a peaceful afternoon at sunset.

Numerous other details enforce the allegory. The reader is left with the impression that in *Joanna and Ulysses,* the author has attempted to produce a work of art comparable to Joanna's paintings—simple and bare to the point of austerity. There are no richly complex characters like Edward Cavan and Carryl Cope, and Joanna herself is interesting but not difficult to understand, since only one aspect of her life is touched upon—her recovery of her "real self." To achieve this, she must be alone, as she is for most of the story, except for a nonhuman companion. All of her conversations give the effect of an inner dialogue with herself. So she becomes a symbol of the human being who, not quite at Dante's midpoint of life, is aware of the need to make a journey—the journey to a spiritual rebirth. With that rebirth comes the power of communion with others; for the first time since her mother's death, Joanna is able to talk freely with her father. Because of its concern with communion, the book is akin to the other novels of Miss Sarton's second group.

Miss Pickthorn and Mr. Hare is regarded by the author as a fable, perhaps because the main characters' names and personalities suggest animals. Miss Pickthorn is a "maiden porcupine" who wants to be left alone. After years of teaching Latin and coping with people, she cherishes her privacy, spends her days translating Horace, and greets uninvited guests with a curt dismissal: "'No doubt we met in some former incarnation, but *not,* I am sure, in this one. I am very busy this morning'" (10). Trumbull Hare, easily frightened by people and civilization, is like some shy woodland creature. When the story opens, he had just moved into an abandoned henhouse that he furnishes with discards from the village rubbish pit; he finds an old iron cot, a stuffed deer's head—all sorts of treasures. Such collecting is not "work" (he fears and avoids conventional jobs) but great pleasure. Nobody interferes with him; and Harry, the road agent, even helps him carry home things too large to balance on his bicycle. But, although Mr. Hare is quiet and attends to his own business, Miss Pickthorn resents his being in the henhouse. To her, he seems "feckless"; and she goes to the selectmen to protest their allowing a hobo to live in the village. His house, she says, is a fire hazard. Although the selectmen promise nothing, she cannot rest until Hare has been removed.

But not only the risk of fire disturbs her: Mr. Hare upsets her unaccountably. Her curiosity about him grows, and she cannot work. She feels "bewitched" and keeps watching his house across the road, with its curl of smoke rising peaceably from the chimney, and she imagines meeting him. When Seth tells her that Mr. Hare had once worked in the mill but had left because he could not stand machines, she gets a new insight into his character.

The climax comes when two pranksters decide to drop a firecracker down Mr. Hare's chimney, and Miss Pickthorn gets out the shotgun (that she keeps handy for scaring away woodchucks) and forces them to stop. There is a great deal of noise when she makes them explode the firecracker in the road; and poor Mr. Hare, just returning from the dump, takes to his heels in alarm. Harry goes to the woods to find him and tell him what has happened. That night the first snow falls, and the next morning Miss Pickthorn, going to her mailbox, meets Mr. Hare on his way to get water. They are like "two solitary polar bears" (78) in the snow; they exchange a few courteous words. But it is their only encounter, for the next day Mr. Hare leaves the village. Seth thinks he has gone because he cannot stand having had his life saved, but more probably he has found the henhouse inadequate protection in the great snow.

At any rate, he vanishes; and again Miss Pickthorn is strangely upset. He has meant something that she cannot, until the end of the book, decipher. But she begins to understand his significance when she finds a small box he has left her; it is a box that once contained peppermints, and inside is a penciled note from Mr. Hare, reading, " 'Thought you might like this little box to keep something in. Hope it wasn't you threw it away!' " (90). This odd memento tells her why Mr. Hare has managed to cast a kind of magic spell over her and over the village, "making them feel for a while as if they were all part of some heroic dream" (90–91). The reason is that Trumbull Hare lives "inside poetry" all the time. He has the poet's or the child's sharp awareness of the world and its strange, unexpected beauties. He will never be dulled by commercialism or by conformity to a pattern. As she returns to her house with the peppermint box, she feels her world is made new, for she now understands poetry better than she ever did in all her years of translating Horace.

As in *Joanna and Ulysses*, the characters in *Miss Pickthorn and Mr. Hare* are extremely simplified, even stylized. Both of the main actors in the tale are elderly people who illustrate the idea that in old age it is possible to escape from some of the conventions and become supremely oneself.

The very unconventionality of Mr. Hare's life in the village interests the inhabitants in him. Without realizing it, Mr. Hare shows the ordinary man, like Seth the postman, what poetry is all about: "Seth was well aware that almost everyone in the village lived a life of wild dream, the dreams of the lonely and the confined. One did not have to tell him that Trumbull Hare had, in a way, opened a door for them all into adventure, into a wilderness they thought they wanted to keep at bay" (88–89). The poet in Mr. Hare accepts the fact of a "wilderness" in life and in people; and in similar way, Miss Pickthorn, who has studied the Latin poets for years, comes to accept Mr. Hare and to realize that he has taught her a great deal about the magic of poetry. After she has "saved" his life, thus openly admitting her covert liking of the man that she has called a hobo, she sees that she and Mr. Hare are really much alike; he is an example of qualities she admires—"hard work, independence, thrift, courage"; in fact, he seems to exemplify these traits more than she does herself. Her complete change of heart shows that one aspect of poetry's magic is its appeal to the essential humanity linking the most opposite of people.

Janet Malcolm, in a review in *The New Yorker*, says that the change in Miss Pickthorn is the focal point in the book since it is "a fable about the function of poetry," for "what has happened is in a sense what happens to a person when he is reading a poem. He sees things in a different light." This reviewer also distinguishes between poetry and fiction as she discusses Miss Sarton's achievement in the book, saying that where fiction deals with "choices and clashes," poetry's realm is in "matters that there is no choice about and no arguing about." After discussion of the author's characters (not taken, she says, from the animal world, but from English novels; for Miss Pickthorn is "the conventional prickly old spinster," and Hare is "the conventional romantic misfit—tramp, free spirit") and the climactic change in Miss Pick-thorn, this reviewer returns to the difference between fiction and poetry: "The question that occupies the novelist—how shall we live?—is parried by the poet, whose subject is the fact that we all must die. The issues that divide the Miss Pickthorns and Mr. Hares of life and of novels simply don't exist in poetry, and this is the moral of the fable." [8]

As in *Joanna and Ulysses,* so in Miss Sarton's third short novel, *The Poet and the Donkey,* (1969), a donkey plays an important part in a person's spiritual development. This time the chief character is Andy Lightfoot, an elderly poet who has lost his Muse. When the story opens, he is disconsolate. For the past three years, his poems have been inspired by Miss Hornbeam, a charming but inaccessible college administrator who caught his imagination when he gave a poetry reading at her college. Like several embodiments of the muse in *Mrs. Stevens Hears the Mermaids Singing,* Miss Hornbeam has been unaware of her magnetic influence on Andy—unaware that his being able to communicate with her now and then has flooded him with happiness and made it possible for him to write poems. Her continued silence and the difficulty he has in telephoning her finally cut off the rich source of creative power.

In his despair he borrows Whiffenpoof, a donkey at a farm near his village, for the summer. Though Whiffenpoof does not become another Muse, caring for her gives Andy a new interest in life; and gradually, as her arthritic ankles are helped by medicine and she becomes again frisky and unpredictable, Andy begins to regain a sense of his real self that has been lost in grieving about Miss Hornbeam. Whiffenpoof's antics—she forms the habit of running away every afternoon at four o'clock—restore his energy and joy. He leaves the impossible dream of Miss Hornbeam's love and returns to reality.

He also returns to charity. Near the end of the story, Mrs. Packer, a wealthy summer resident of the village, brings him some of his books to autograph and while there helps to catch Whiffen-poof, just returned from one of her daily sprints. As Andy and Mrs. Packer talk, he realizes that he has long had a stereotyped idea of her as someone rich and aloof. Instead, she is as vulnerable as himself: "He sensed that behind the matronly figure, the heavy jowls and the tight little mouth, she was full of tremors, a very delicate and sensitive machine, afraid of its own power to register distant earthquakes" (110). During this short visit, they feel a kinship. They are both growing old, and they both have suffered. As Mrs. Packer had lost her maternal role when her son died, so Andy had lost his sense of himself as a poet when Miss Hornbeam withdrew.

The Poet and the Donkey, set in the same New Hampshire village where Miss Pickthorn and Mr. Hare live, is similar to the previous tale in its simplicity of plot and its delicate humor. The spectacle of the elderly poet running down the road after a donkey and feeling exhilarated by the chase is as amusing as Trumbull Hare's enjoying life in his henhouse, or Miss Pickthorn's brandishing a shotgun. In both tales the serious subject—the value of poetry in the world—is just below the humorous surface, never made too obvious but always kept in view.

A comparison of *The Poet and the Donkey* to *Mrs. Stevens Hears the Mermaids Singing* can also be made; in both, the creative process is seen as the outcome of love, an intensity and excitement arising from attachment to a person who is the embodiment of the muse. But Andy Lightfoot comes to a deeper understanding of poetry than Mrs. Stevens has. Through his care of the donkey he finds that inspiration can come from giving of oneself and not just from waiting for a word from the muse. Whiffenpoof is to him a "magic animal" (119) who makes everyone around her seem more likeable; but it is Andy's own demanding self that has become, through the experience with Whiffenpoof, less egoistic and more human. In discovering that he can write poetry without his inacessible Muse, he takes a step forward on his spiritual journey.

V *Kinds of Love* (1970)

Miss Sarton's latest full-length novel, *Kinds of Love*, is again set in New Hampshire, and has some characters similar to those in her other novels. But it is distinctly different from all the others. As the story opens, Christina and Cornelius Chapman, who for years have spent their summers in the small town of Willard, decide to spend the winter there for the first time; for Cornelius is recovering from a stroke, and their whole pattern of life must change. Christina's best friend in Willard is Ellen Comstock, a native of the town, whose grown son, Nick, returned from World War II unnerved to the point of mental instability.

At the beginning of the novel, when Christina and Ellen take a walk through the woods, the reader learns of their affection for each other and also of the tension between them because Ellen has always been poor and very conscious of Christina's different social world. Their friendship goes back to childhood, but as a young woman Christina was so involved in college, parties in Boston, and trips to Europe that she saw little of Ellen. On the autumn day of their walk, they are observed by Old Pete, the town "character," a cheerful ne'er-do-well who lives in a shack and knows all the woods and trails around Willard.

Plans are going forward in Willard for the celebration of its bicentennial in 1969, and both Ellen and Christina are asked to write chapters for the town history. At a meeting of citizens planning the bicentennial, the reader becomes acquainted with Jane Tuttle, a charming elderly lady who specializes in natural history; Jem Grindell, the town historian; Susie Plummer, a retired missionary who is now the librarian; and Sally and Timothy Webster, summer residents.

When the hunting season begins, Ellen is increasingly worried about Nick, who has an obsession about wild life and cannot bear the thought of any woodland creature being killed. Accompanied by Old Pete, he sets out one afternoon to throw some New Yorkers off the trail of a deer. But the hunters have wounded the deer, and Nick, after mercifully killing it, gets into a fight with the men who claim it. As the incident occurs on the Chapman property, Cornelius accuses both the strangers and Nick of trespassing. Christina, not wanting to upset Cornelius but anxious about her relationship with Ellen, goes to ask advice of Eben Fifield, a former admirer of hers who, since his wife's death, has lived alone in Willard. Eben suggests someone who can handle the matter out of court, and gradually all resentment of Nick is forgotten, especially since he is—apart from his sudden rages concerning wild life —a most gentle, kindly man. When the winter begins, Nick comes to shovel snow and carry in wood for Christina and Cornelius.

The first section of the novel ends with the Chapman children and grandchildren coming to the Ark, the family home at Willard, for Thanksgiving. John, the eldest, who is subject to moods of great depression, goes to visit Jane Tuttle, who enlists his help with her chapter on the natural history of Willard. At the Thanksgiving dinner they all discuss what the town has meant to them over the years.

In Part II, winter sets in with great snowfalls. Christina takes Cornelius to the doctor in Boston and learns that his hold on life is precarious but that his illness may go on for years. She herself, with a stiff knee, is finding the household work more than she can manage, and Ellen kindly offers to come twice a week to help her. Both of them are writing their chapters for the town history, and the reader learns about early schools in Willard and about how a group of women and children managed on their own when their men were away in the Civil War. In mid-winter Jane Tuttle dies and is mourned by everyone. After the funeral Christina invites Eben to call at the Ark, and he and Cornelius have a long talk; it is the beginning of a real friendship between the former rivals. Old Pete is taken to the hospital with both feet frozen.

In the late winter, Cathy, one of the grandchildren, comes to live with Christina and Cornelius and go to high school in Willard, as she has been unhappy in her Boston school. She brings new life into the Ark. She also is fond of Ellen, with whom she can have real conversations, such as are impossible with her own parents. One night a Dartmouth student, Joel Smith, wrecks his car near the Comstock house, and Ellen and Nick take him in. Having no wish to return to college, he remains with them during the spring. Nick and Cathy between them teach Joel much about animals, birds, and flowers, and he comes to appreciate the peace and welcome of Willard. He and Cathy fall in love.

One day when Nick and Joel are walking in the woods, the road agent comes along with a bulldozer, ready to widen a part of the road to accommodate snow plows the next winter. The place to be cut is especially beautiful with wild arbutus, and Nick is furious at the impending destruction. Before Joel can stop him, he strikes the road agent, who threatens to send him to jail. When Ellen learns of the fight, she decides that the time has come to take Nick back to the state hospital, where he had spent some years just after the war. On the same night that Joel drives them to the hospital, he has dinner at the Ark, and the next day he leaves to begin his two-year military training. Soon his long letters to Cathy begin to come, and she writes dozens of poems about their love.

But as the weeks pass she begins to feel she is changing, falling "out of love"; she is miserable with uncertainty.

The last section of the novel describes the celebration of the bicentennial, at which Eben Fifield gives a magnificent speech showing the continuity of past and present and seeing the town as a creation of many people.

A summary of the plot of *Kinds of Love* cannot do justice to its complexity. In its variety of themes and breadth of vision, it stands apart from all of Miss Sarton's previous novels.

It is notable for its sympathetic portrayal of many types of personality. All of the Chapman clan are seen together only once, at Thanksgiving; but the reader gets a clear picture of each one and feels something of the problems, relationships, and activities that will be continued after they all leave the scene. In the same way, the townspeople, such as Jem Grindell, the Websters, and Old Pete—all minor characters—are felt as real people, who together make up the great diversity of life in Willard. As in all of Miss Sarton's novels, the thoughts, feelings, and interaction of the characters are more important than any external action. And the town itself, with its "raggedy weeds and stony pastures" (464) is like another character, influencing and being influenced by all those who have ever lived there. In addition, much of the novel's interest comes from the reader's awareness of the dead—Cornelius' father, Ellen's husband, and, further back, Sophia Dole, who in Civil War days was in charge of the group of women who kept the town going while the men were fighting.

Unlike many of Miss Sarton's other novels, *Kinds of Love* does not emphasize a need for communion. Rather, it shows communion being achieved—not perfectly, of course, but more nearly so than in any of the previous novels. It is achieved sometimes by a look or a handclasp between two people who love each other; sometimes by silence, like that between John Chapman and old Jane Tuttle, who have been friends for years. Ellen and Nick usually understand each other without words. The most nearly perfect communion in the book is between Christina and her husband, who find that in old age they know each other better and that their love is growing stronger. Christina says in one of the journal entries interspersed in the narrative: "in all these weeks, we have moved into a deepening phase where we are closer as souls than ever before" (251).

The love of Christina and Cornelius is tenderly and beautifully portrayed. Christina delights in their isolation in the winter; she even dreads the coming of Cathy in the spring, as the absence of visitors has meant a chance to be alone with Cornelius in a way not possible before. Paradoxically, they are happiest with each other at a time when they might have expected only sadness. Their "second honeymoon" is the result of Cornelius' illness and of their both being aware of the nearness of death. Cornelius marvels that he can now live without the bank and his club, things that formerly seemed essential. He says, " 'Other things have come to the surface. We are in a great adventure, Christina. . . . I am a better man than I was a year ago, a richer man, a . . . happier man. How strange!' " (234).

Eben Fifield also finds that love in old age is still vital. He and Christina still light up each other as they did in their twenties. After his speech at the bicentennial, he tells her, " 'Between you and me there is fire. There always was and there always will be. It burned so brightly today that I hardly dared look at you from the platform. Yet because you were there, and I so aware of your presence, the thing worked' " (451). Though both of them have been happily married and would not change what has been in the past, they accept a truth that strikes Eben as a sudden revelation: " 'What is young love compared to this—this incomparable truth of old age—that nothing dies, all is transformed?' " (452).

Another kind of love explored in the novel is that between friends. Christina and Ellen, so different in background and temperament, are alike in tastes and values and are a constant comfort and joy to each other. Their relationship is so close that it can endure strains and only becomes stronger for them. Another deep friendship is that between John Chapman, a middle-aged man who often feels himself a failure, and gentle, elderly Jane Tuttle. Since he was four years old and they went for walks together, they have felt an affinity arising from their love of the natural world, and Jane has been able to give John something very precious, a sense of his real, inner self.

A love of nature pervades the novel. It is seen in an extreme, obsessive form in Nick Comstock, who is called a one-man conservation society. Joel Smith thinks Nick a saint because of his selfless caring for every wild creature; but Ellen, with typical clear-sighted realism, says, " 'It isn't saintly to my way of thinking to care more about animals than people' " (458). Nick's concern, how-ever, affects everyone in the town. And other characters besides Jane Tuttle and John are moved by the natural beauty of the wild country around Willard. The Chapmans turn again and again to the mountain, Monadnock, for reassurance and joy. Joel, the city boy, is entranced by the delicate beauty of the wild arbutus in spring. And Miss Sarton's own love of New England pervades the book. One reviewer said:

> Most of all, the novel concerns the reciprocal love between man-kind and nature: the love that the earth gives to those capable of taking its pulse and the love that human beings give to nature when they are close enough to receive its love. A New Hampshire village is the brooding alma mater, with its tempers of winter, bursting joy of spring, laziness of summer and flaming last vivid flair of fall. Only a poet—and May Sarton is a poet—could translate into words the special relationship that prevails between the time-lessness of the earth and the evanescence of the creatures, great and small, which live upon it.[9]

Other kinds of love are woven into the intricate texture of the novel: the young love of Cathy and Joel; the almost wordless love of Ellen for her child, Nick; the concern of the townspeople for one another, as shown in the care for Old Pete; and the love of people for Willard—its past history and its future. Those who work for the bicentennial celebration begin to see the relationship of the "summer people" to the natives—how these two groups, often considered antagonistic, actually have given much to each other. Cornelius, who had formerly thought of the summer residents as being the "civilizing influence" (240) in the town, comes, through his new knowledge of Eben, Ellen and Nick, to respect the intel-ligence and integrity of people who have never left Willard.

Ellen Comstock has the toughness characteristic of those who remained in Willard. Her problems—poverty, an alcoholic hus-band, and a mentally unstable son—have made her realistic but not bitter. She can comfort Cathy, who is fifteen, and Christina, who is seventy. She represents all the women of Willard who, in the words of Old Pete, "'have been given a grain or two more pluck than the men'" (17).

Kinds of Love is also a novel about kinds of courage. Young Cathy and Joel bring to the town a greater awareness of materialism, injustice, and war, all of which demand courage. But the problems of old age are treated in more detail: the loneliness of Ellen, stitching away at other people's sewing, and of Eben, standing in the garden on an autumn day and knowing he should cut down the peonies as his wife always did; the frailty and dependence that Jane Tuttle must live with; Christina's knowledge that Cornelius may soon die. All of these are faced with courage. Miss Sarton shows her elderly characters as not only able to achieve communion but as also able to endure.

In its variety of themes and characters, then, *Kinds of Love* is richer than any of Miss Sarton's previous novels. It marks a peak of achievement, for it depicts more than one town and its people. A reviewer who commented on the novel's containing "so much of what life is" also saw the wider implication of the story: "Miss Sarton's book, despite the setting, is not purely about a New England village. It is about the world. She finds the macrocosm in the microcosm of Willard and she makes us see it, too." [10]

CHAPTER 5

Conclusion: The Inner Journey

IN *Plant Dreaming Deep*, Miss Sarton speaks of her disappointment with the critical reception of her work and adds: "I believe that eventually my work will be seen as a whole, all the poems and all the novels, as the expression of a vision of life which, though unfashionable all the way, has validity . . ." (91). Like most good authors, she continues to write, and therefore the vision of life is still incomplete; but it is possible to define more succinctly than the preceding chapters have done the nature of her achievement.

One of her greatest gifts, in both the poetry and the novels, is in so describing the world of external nature that the reader is made keenly aware of its quality—its beauty, poignancy, harshness, gentleness. The world is loved in all its moods: heat and drought, the rustling and tinkling sounds of summer, the weight and brilliance of snow. Every volume of poetry contains some treatment of nature in fresh, perceptive images and her characteristic subtle music. Her depiction of the New England scene is comparable to that of Robert Frost, for in both poetry and prose she shows keen perception and a love of the countryside that is untainted by sentimentality. In the novels, places rather than people catch the reader's imagination: Dene's Court in Ireland; Paris; the Harvard University campus; and Belgian gardens such as Doro's and the Duchesnes', with their white tables and chairs under the apple trees. Interestingly, a similar comment could be made about another poet-novelist, Thomas Hardy, whose characters are, for the most part, less compelling than his places. (His Michael Henchard, whose character is dominant, is comparable to Miss Sarton's Edward Cavan; both attain heroic stature through suffering.)

The principal idea in Miss Sarton's work is the need to be oneself. The individual must not "give up his differences," says Doro in the first novel, *The Single Hound*; and the latest novel, *Kinds of Love*, emphasizes the unique value of every human being. A situation occurring in three of the early novels is that of a young person who mistakenly tries to "take over" an older person's life and experience instead of building his own: Mark Taylor tries in *The Single Hound* to break into Georgia's life with the violence of his emotion; Francis Chabrier in *Shadow of a Man*, and Sally, in *A Shower of Summer Days*, long for the confidence and emotional power of an older person—they want to be a part of a richness already achieved and so resist, at first, the need to experience life in their own way. Miss Sarton is particularly concerned, in all the novels, with the life of women—their need to achieve selfhood in their own right, not to lose it in their identification with the men they love. The difficulty of being a woman, fulfilling the multifarious demands made on her and yet keeping her integrity and identity, is seen in the stories of Frances Wyeth, Melanie Duchesne, Solange Bernard, and Violet Dene Gordon (to mention only the most obvious examples); and in the poetry the theme is touched on most specifically in "My Sisters, O My Sisters."

Throughout her work, Miss Sarton shows the importance of emotion. She dislikes the fear of feeling that she finds in the modern world, for to feel is to be human, and emotion should not be denied or covered up. Sprig Wyeth (in *Birth of a Grandfather*), afraid that he will lose some essential part of himself if he gives way to emotion; Carryl Cope (*The Small Room*), afraid of her own intensity; all of the "safe," restrained New Englanders pictured in *Shadow of a Man* and *Faithful Are the Wounds*—these depict a denial of the human heritage. Joanna and her father (in *Joanna and Ulysses*) learn that when they shut away painful memories, they are shutting out life itself. It is better to be like Doro in *The Single Hound*, who tries to "grasp anguish and by holding it close, make it hers"; for "To possess pain completely seemed one way of conquering it" (12). Painful emotion can thus be transcended but should never be denied. The intensity of fiery people like Dante, Erasmus, and Edmund Burke is praised, not only in the specific poems that mention them ("The Sacred Order" and "Not Always the Quiet Word"), but in the general tenor of all the poetry.

One of the great values of strong feeling, as seen in the two poems just mentioned, is that since it is often creative, it can bring about change in the culture and can produce the work of art. In her theory of poetry, Miss Sarton makes clear that, when emotional force is channeled into art, there is some loss to the artist as a person. As early as 1939, in poems of *Inner Landscape*, she had the poet renounce personal desire in order to perfect his art; for art was a supreme value in itself. As a young writer, she was fascinated by the difference between art and life; and in *Mrs. Stevens*, the characters discuss the same subject—the nebulous, fleeting quality of life as opposed to the stillness and permanence of art. Is art, then, to be preferred to life? The question is never really answered in Miss Sarton's work; but she shows, especially in the novels, that the quality of detachment, so necessary to the artist, is also a means of personal growth. Character is created somewhat as a poem is. So perhaps the artist's loss of personal satisfaction is actually his gain.

As in the creation of art, the creation of character is best accomplished if emotion is highly valued; for only those who feel strongly are capable of real detachment. A first step in growth, suggested in both the poems and the novels, is to recognize that passion and love are not the same. Passion, the energizing force, is good, but it leads to pain and to a kind of death unless it can be transcended. The theme of one section of the collected poems, "Leaves Before the Wind," is that passionate love, which seems so rich and absolute, also means conflict, inevitable parting, despair. The bleak images of *Inner Landscape* suggest this violent pain, as does the memorable image in *The Lion and the Rose* of the lovers standing immobile, "Like two Sebastians, pierced, and hand in hand." Mark Taylor, in *The Single Hound*, and Francis Chabrier, in *Shadow of a Man*, know this anguish; but they also begin to understand detachment, which means growth in charity and real communion. They have started the inner journey toward a greater humanity.

The need for love, as distinct from passion, is emphasized in all the novels. Love, which can relieve the painful sense of separateness felt by all people, is seen in *The Bridge of Years* as "positive detachment," the quality indicated by T. S. Eliot in the line "Teach us to care and not to care." This delicate balance is finally understood by Paul Duchesne, who, in giving up anxiety about his reputation and writing with love, succeeds where he had hitherto failed. Edward Cavan (of *Faithful Are the Wounds*), on the other hand, is the character who "cares" most intensely of all those in Miss Sarton's fiction; yet he cannot be detached—he cannot learn how "not to care." Sprig Wyeth *(Birth of a Grandfather)* has trouble in communicating for the opposite reason: his selfishness, which comes from a lack of imagination, keeps him from caring enough. Always, if the fervent individual learns detachment, greater communion is possible; love is then released to bless the world. This love is called in *The Land of Silence* "a point of burning far from passion." In general, the early poems that treat communion with or a love of a mankind are too direct or declamatory to be effective. The later ones of *A Private Mythology* and *A Grain of Mustard Seed*, however, suggest more subtly a love of all creation; they imply that such love involves a willingness to suffer and produces, in the end, a kind of rebirth of the individual.

The emphasis on rebirth in Miss Sarton's poetry and prose is akin to the need for greater life that is a theme in much other modern literature. Is her work, then, really "unfashionable" as Miss Sarton has said? It is, in the sense that it offers no problems to the reader and is optimistic in its general tone. The modern temper is one of distrust of whatever is pleasurable and comfortable. Greater life is believed to come from rejection of traditional values and from difficulty and struggle—the reader's difficulty in understanding the work of art, and the characters' painful struggles for self-affirmation. Because Miss Sarton's works can be easily understood, they have perhaps not been taken seriously by most critics. But possibly also these critics, seeing no obscurity, do not pause long enough to examine her "deceptive clarity." The delicate nuances of her sound effects in the poetry are paralleled by the quietness with which her keenest perceptions are detailed in her novels. The characters in the novels and the persona of the poems understand anguish, but their inner struggles do not, except in the case of Edward Cavan, manifest themselves in overt acts. Her novels contain no melodrama or horror—no murder, rape, incest, or torture—yet both they and the poems show not only a scrupulous examination of belief, conscience, and feeling, but also a sharp awareness of suffering. Still, although the idea of a psychic energy released by pain is present in her works, there is no deliberate seeking of "unpleasure" [1] by any of her characters. For such reasons it must be concluded that her work is not in the mainstream of modern literature.

But her work is not thereby negligible. The word "civilized" has been applied to her poetry and used in both blame and praise. One reviewer of *A Private Mythology* called the book "cultivated rather than worldly, tasteful, civilized, and accomplished," adding that today no writer wants to have such adjectives applied to him since they indicate qualities that "no longer have value in literature." [2] But another reviewer has compared Miss Sarton's poetry to that of W. H. Auden, in that both exhibit a "civilized and intricate way to see." [3] And James Dickey, writing in *The Sewanee Review*, says of her, "In almost every poem she attains a delicate simplicity as quickeningly direct as it is deeply given, and does so with the courteous serenity, the clear, caring, and intelligent human calm of the queen of a small well-ordered country." [4]

Clearly, the writer who suggests a means of ordering man's inner and outer chaos still has something to say to the modern reader, whether or not an emphasis on order is considered unfashionable. And such emphasis is prominent in her work. The poet works with his own emotional chaos and with the multiple images that flood his mind and eventually brings forth the ordered form of the work of art. So the individual can work with pain, fear, passion, and the anguish of the world he lives in; and by doing so he can achieve greater humanity, make of himself someone more available to the needs of his time. To be civilized, Miss Sarton is saying, is to use intellect and imagination to free the individual from the dark forces of selfishness and chaos.

Related to the praise of order in her work is the persistent idea of reclaiming or restoring what has been lost or diminished. Her own house in New Hampshire, restored to its original grace, stands as a kind of symbol of other restorations: Jacques, the war-sick soldier, saved from despondency and sloth by Melanie; Ulysses, the donkey, healed by Joanna; Dene's Court opened after twenty years, scrubbed and aired, and made the center of life again; Mr. Hare finding beauty and value in things long since discarded. A characteristic occupation of many of Miss Sarton's heroines is weeding the garden; it provides an outlet for pent-up emotion and at the same time makes for order. And, in *A Private Mythology*, the poem "The Walled Garden at Clondalkin" stands as a pattern of the theme of restoration. It tells of a beautiful garden fallen into ruin, "destroyed, invaded, overgrown," that is reclaimed by a hired man:

Not even a relative, poor, and of no fame,
A water-carrier, trundler of wheelbarrows.
Quiet and slow, his pockets full of seeds,
He cleared the wild disordered past of weeds.

With his "patient human ways," bringing back what had been lost, he seems a symbol of the values set forth in Miss Sarton's work. Her belief is in man and in cultural continuity with the past, in order and beauty, in all that characterizes the great humanistic tradition.

Notes and References

Chapter One

1. "The School of Babylon," in *The Moment of Poetry*, ed. Don Cameron Allen (Baltimore, 1962), pp. 27–47.
2. "A Country Incident," *A Private Mythology* (New York, 1966), p. 77.
3. *The Lion and the Rose* (New York, 1948), pp. 85–86.
4. "The School of Babylon," p. 31.
5. *The Lion and the Rose*, pp. 83–84.
6. *Ibid.*, p. 77.
7. *The Land of Silence* (New York, 1953), p. 17.
8. *Ibid.*, pp. 22–23.
9. Dust jacket of *The Lion and the Rose.*
10. *The Lion and the Rose*, pp.30–36.
11. *Cloud, Stone, Sun, Vine* (New York, 1961), p. 135.
12. *As Does New Hampshire* (Peterborough, New Hampshire, 1967), pp. 14–15.

Chapter Two

1. William Rose Benét, "The Phoenix Nest," *Saturday Review of Literature*, XV (March 27, 1937), 18.
2. In *The Observer* (London), April 2, 1939.
3. *Ibid.*
4. Ray Smith, "The Rose and the Oration," review of *The Lion and the Rose* (New York, 1948), *Poetry: A Magazine of Verse*, LXXIII (Feb., 1949), 292–93.
5. Robert Hazel, "Three New Volumes," *Poetry: A Magazine of Verse*, XCIV (Aug., 1959), 343–45.
6. Joseph Bennett, "Indian, Greek and Japanese," New York *Times Book Review*, Nov. 13, 1966, p. 6.
7. "Der Abschied," *Cloud, Stone, Sun, Vine* (New York, 1961), pp. 143–44.
8. Dust jacket of *Cloud, Stone, Sun, Vine.*
9. May Sarton, *The Writing of a Poem*, Scripps College Bulletin, XXXI, 2 (Feb., 1957), 2.

10. *Ibid.,* p. 17.

11. "The School of Babylon," *The Moment of Poetry,* ed. Don Cameron Allen (Baltimore, 1962), pp. 27–47.

12. "Binding the Dragon," *In Time Like Air* (New York, 1957), p. 61.

13. *The Land of Silence,* (New York, 1953), p. 93.

14. "On Growth and Change," the third article in a series on "The Poet and His Work," *The Christian Science Monitor,* March 16, 1966, p. 12.

15. Dust jacket of *Mrs. Stevens Hears the Mermaids Singing* (New York, 1965).

16. *The Land of Silence,* p. 90.

17. "A Poet's Letter to a Beginner," *The Writer,* LXXV (April, 1962), 19–21.

18. "On Growth and Change."

19. *The Writing of a Poem,* p. 20.

20. *Ibid.*

21. "On Growth and Change."

22. *Ibid.*

23. "These Pure Arches," *The Lion and the Rose,* p. 81.

24. *The Writing of a Poem,* p. 5.

25. "A Poet's Letter to a Beginner."

26. "Foreword," *Beloit Poetry Journal,* I, 1 (Fall, 1950), 3–5.

27. "The School of Babylon."

28. "After a Train Journey," *The Lion and the Rose,* p. 44.

19. Martha Bacon, "Marvels of Interwoven Syllables," review of *The Lion and the Rose, Saturday Review of Literature,* XXXI (April 17, 1948), 50.

Chapter Three

1. Frank Swinnerton in *The Observer* (London), April 24, 1938; and Jane Spence Southron in New York *Times Book Review,* March 20, 1938, p. 6.

2. L. P. Hartley in *The Sketch* (London), May 11, 1938.

3. May Sarton, *The Design of a Novel,* Scripps College Bulletin, XXXVII, 4 (July, 1963),6–7.

4. *Ibid.,* p. 6

Chapter Four

1. *Cloud, Stone, Sun, Vine,* p. 119.

2. *The Design of a Novel,* Scripps College Bulletin, pp. 6–7.

3. William Goyen, "A Craving for Light," review of *Faithful Are the Wounds,* New York *Times Book Review,* March 13, 1955, p. 6.

4. *The Design of a Novel*, p. 14.

5. *Ibid.*

6. Goyen, *loc. cit.*

7. In "Ash Wednesday," *T. S. Eliot, The Complete Poems and Plays* (New York, 1952), pp. 60–67.

8. Janet Malcolm, "Children's Books for Christmas," *The New Yorker*, XLII(Dec. 17, 1966), 210–40.

9. Fanny Butcher, "A Poet's Novel," review of *Kinds of Love*, Chicago *Tribune*, Dec. 25, 1970.

10. Eugenia Thornton, "The World in New Hampshire," review of *Kinds of Love*, Cleveland *Plain Dealer*, Nov. 29, 1970.

Chapter Five

1. A term used by Lionel Trilling, quoting Freud, in *Beyond Culture* (New York, 1965), p. 72.

2. Constance Urdang, "Gregor, Sarton, Vazakas," *Poetry: A Magazine of Verse*, CXII (April, 1968), 44–48.

3. Robert Hazel, "Three New Volumes," *Poetry: A Magazine of Verse*, XCIV (Aug., 1959), 343–45.

4. James Dickey, "In the Presence of Anthologies," *Sewanee Review*, LXVI (Spring, 1958), 294–314.

Selected Bibliography

PRIMARY SOURCES

A. *Books*

Encounter in April. Boston: Houghton Mifflin Co., 1937.
The Single Hound. Boston: Houghton Mifflin Co., 1938.
Inner Landscape. Boston: Houghton Mifflin Co., 1939.
The Bridge of Years. New York: Doubleday and Co., 1946.
The Lion and the Rose. New York: Rinehart and Co., 1948.
Shadow of a Man. New York: Rinehart and Co., 1950.
A Shower of Summer Days. New York: Rinehart and Co., 1952.
The Land of Silence. New York: Rinehart and Co., 1953.
Faithful Are the Wounds. New York: Rinehart and Co., 1955.
The Fur Person. New York: Rinehart and Co., 1956. (Reissued by
    W. W. Norton and Co., 1968.)
The Birth of a Grandfather. New York: Rinehart and Co., 1957.
In Time Like Air. New York: Rinehart and Co., 1958.
I Knew a Phoenix. New York: Rinehart and Co., 1959. (Reissued by
    W. W. Norton and Co., 1969.)
Cloud, Stone, Sun, Vine. New York: W. W. Norton and Co., 1961.
The Small Room. New York: W. W. Norton and Co., 1961.
Joanna and Ulysses. New York: W. W. Norton and Co., 1964.
Mrs. Stevens Hears the Mermaids Singing. New York: W. W. Norton
    and Co., 1965.
Miss Pickthorn and Mr. Hare. New York: W. W. Norton and Co.,
    1966.
A Private Mythology. New York: W. W. Norton and Co., 1966.
Plant Dreaming Deep. New York: W. W. Norton and Co., 1967.
As Does New Hampshire. Peterborough, New Hampshire: R. R. Smith
    Co., 1967.
The Poet and the Donkey. New York: W. W. Norton and Co., 1969.
Kinds of Love. New York: W. W. Norton and Co., 1970.
A Grain of Mustard Seed. New York: W. W. Norton and Co., 1971.
A Durable Fire. New York: W. W. Norton and Co., 1972.

B. *Articles and Monographs*

"Foreword," *Beloit Poetry Journal*, I, 1 (Fall, 1950), 3–5.
The Writing of a Poem, Scripps College Bulletin, XXXI, 2 (Feb., 1957).
"A Poet's Letter to a Beginner," *The Writer*, LXXV (April, 1962), 19–21.
"The School of Babylon," in *The Moment of Poetry*, ed. Don Cameron Allen. Baltimore: The Johns Hopkins Press, 1962.
The Design of a Novel, Scripps College Bulletin, XXXVII, 4 (July, 1963).
"On Growth and Change," *The Christian Science Monitor*, March 16, 1966, p. 12.
"Homeward," twelve monthly articles, *Family Circle*, June, 1968– June, 1969.

SECONDARY SOURCES

BACON, MARTHA. "Marvels of Interwoven Syllables," review of *The Lion and the Rose*, *Saturday Review of Literature*, XXXI (April 17, 1948), 50. Fine treatment of the poet's diction and form.
BENÉT, WILLIAM ROSE. "The Phoenix Nest," *Saturday Review of Literature*, XV (March 27, 1937), 18. Perceptive comment on *Encounter in April*; sees it as a work of extraordinary promise.
BENNETT, JOSEPH. "Indian, Greek and Japanese," review of *A Private Mythology*, New York *Times Book Review*, Nov. 13, 1966, p. 6. Thoughtfully written, with particular appreciation of the poems about India.
BUTCHER, FANNY. "A Poet's Novel," review of *Kinds of Love*, Chicago *Tribune*, Dec. 25, 1970. Enthusiastic discussion, with emphasis on the novel's atmosphere.
DE SELINCOURT, BASIL. Review of *Inner Landscape*, *The Observer* (London), April 2, 1939. Excellent analysis of the poet's ideas and techniques. The comments on the theme of renunciation apply not only to *Inner Landscape* but to much of her other work as well.
DICKEY, JAMES. "In the Presence of Anthologies," *Sewanee Review*, LXVI (Spring, 1958), 294–314. Brief comment on *In Time Like Air*; praises beauty and assurance of the poems.
GOYEN, WILLIAM. "A Craving for Light," review of *Faithful Are the Wounds*, New York *Times Book Review*, March 13, 1955, p. 6. Beautifully written tribute to the artistry and truth of this novel; useful also for its understanding of Miss Sarton's general approach in fiction.

HARTLEY, L. P. Review of *The Single Hound, The Sketch* (London), May 11, 1938. Novel seen as a work that reconciles the sensual and spiritual worlds.

HAZEL, ROBERT. "Three New Volumes," *Poetry: A Magazine of Verse,* XCIV (Aug., 1959), 343–45. Well-balanced, thoughtful review of *In Time Like Air.*

MALCOLM, JANET. "Children's Books for Christmas," *The New Yorker,* XLII (Dec. 17, 1966), 210–40. Sensitive appreciation of *Miss Pickthorn and Mr. Hare,* analyzing it as "a fable about the function of poetry."

SMITH, RAY. "The Rose and the Oration," review of *The Lion and the Rose, Poetry: A Magazine of Verse,* LXIII (Feb., 1949), 292–93. Interesting comments on the poet's symbolism and her lyrics about places.

SWINNERTON, FRANK. Review of *The Single Hound, The Observer* (London), April 24, 1938. While critical of the novel's "preciosity of approach," praises insight into the spirit of the modern world.

THORNTON, EUGENIA. "The World in New Hampshire," review of *Kinds of Love,* Cleveland *Plain Dealer,* Nov. 29, 1970. Perceptive comment on the fullness of life in the novel.

TRILLING, LIONEL. *Beyond Culture.* New York: The Viking Press, 1965. Discussion of a "modern" approach not used in Miss Sarton's work.

URDANG, CONSTANCE. "Gregor, Sarton, Vazakas," *Poetry: A Magazine of Verse,* CXII (April, 1968), 44–48. Sees *A Private Mythology* as old-fashioned.

Index